Let There Be Wisdom In Truth

Let There Be Wisdom In Truth

BY Asif Shakoor

ILLUSTRATIONS BY
Maliha Shakoor, Benjamin Aysan,
and Asif Shakoor

RESOURCE *Publications* · Eugene, Oregon

LET THERE BE WISDOM IN TRUTH

Copyright © 2021 Asif Shakoor. All rights reserved. Except for brief quotations in critical publications or reviews, no part of this book may be reproduced in any manner without prior written permission from the publisher. Write: Permissions, Wipf and Stock Publishers, 199 W. 8th Ave., Suite 3, Eugene, OR 97401.

Resource Publications
An Imprint of Wipf and Stock Publishers
199 W. 8th Ave., Suite 3
Eugene, OR 97401

www.wipfandstock.com

PAPERBACK ISBN: 978-1-6667-0469-3
HARDCOVER ISBN: 978-1-6667-0470-9
EBOOK ISBN: 978-1-6667-0471-6

Contents

1. Introduction
2. Root of Change | 2
3. Winter's Bite | 4
4. Will of Body | 5
5. Eyes Opened | 6
6. Being Born | 6
7. Vanity | 7
8. Trapped in Doubt | 8
9. The Forest Calls | 11
10. Human Greed | 12
11. Hardship | 14
12. Etched Emotions | 14
13. Total Freedom | 15
14. Entropy of Life | 16
15. Death and Life | 18
16. Journey in Time | 20
17. Mind's Illusion | 20
18. Unity of Self | 21
19. Dream World | 21
20. Conscious Stream | 24
21. Silence | 26
22. Etched | 27
23. Liberated | 28
24. Harmony | 29
25. Wings | 29
26. Silent Reflection | 32
27. Spirit in Form | 34
28. Curiosity | 37
29. Limits | 37
30. Fool in Folly | 38
31. Frozen | 39
32. Freed Spirit | 40
33. Move with Time | 42
34. Beauty of Nature | 44
35. Mystical | 44
36. Aged Wisdom | 45
37. Human Mold | 46
38. Perception | 46
39. A Guest Within | 48
40. Oh, Children | 49
41. Fair Wind | 51
42. No Holding Time | 53
43. Neglect | 55
44. Law and Justice | 55
45. Leadership | 56
46. Yet So Near | 57
47. Wisdom in Sorrow | 58
48. Mystical Embrace | 62
49. Hard Reality | 64
50. Lost Path | 66
51. Just Look | 66
52. Life and Death | 67
53. Conscious Veil | 67
54. Drifting in Time | 69
55. Joy in Sorrow | 71
56. Autumn Leaves | 71
57. Conscious Love | 72
58. Nature of Man | 74

Contents

59. Chasing Humanity | 77
60. Mask of Deception | 77
61. Voice of Wisdom | 78
62. Moral Gaze | 78
63. Mystical Love | 79
64. Moral Truth | 80
65. Web of Darkness | 84
66. Open Mind | 86
67. Conscious Dream | 88
68. Of Substance | 90
69. On Fire | 90
70. Deep Ocean | 91
71. Oppressed Freedom | 92
72. A Desert Night | 95
73. All-consuming | 97
74. Waste | 97
75. Journey | 98
76. Well of Greed | 98
77. Humanity | 99
78. The Way Into Tao | 100
79. Happiness | 102
80. Slow Down | 103
81. Etched Moments | 104
82. Wall of Ignorance | 106
83. Morally Strong | 106
84. Enemy of Youth | 107
85. Faith Gives | 108
86. Vigor of Youth | 111
87. How Deep | 114
88. All Will Go | 114
89. Prisoners | 115
90. Life Dance | 115
91. Light of Humanity | 118
92. Words of Silence | 121
93. Gluttony | 122
94. A Guest | 123
95. Human Grace | 124
96. Evil Uprooted | 124
97. Burning Love | 127
98. Heavy Steps | 129
99. Guest for a Day | 129
100. Hasty Steps | 130
101. Shadow in Form | 130
102. Seeking | 131
103. Delusions of Power | 132
104. Breath of Air | 134
105. Virtuous Truth | 137
106. Less Spoken | 137
107. Emotional Reality | 138
108. Silence Breaks | 139
109. Power Over Power | 141
110. Fading Footsteps | 143
111. Blood of Humanity | 145
112. Firm Ground | 145
113. Being True | 146
114. Emotions in Knots | 147
115. No Vision! No Light! | 147
116. Nature of Time | 149
117. The Glass Reality | 152
118. Invisible Web | 154
119. Conscious Eye | 154
120. Eternal Truth | 155
121. One Night | 156
122. Nature Divine | 156
123. Conscious Journey | 158
124. Book of Pages | 160
125. Free Willed | 164
126. Love of Nature | 164
127. Worldly Soul | 165
128. Emotions of Love | 165
129. Nature of Love | 168
130. Blind Vanity | 169
131. Powerless | 170
132. Light Journey | 170
133. Voice of Morality | 171
134. Human Folly | 172
135. Wisdom in Truth | 173

Contents

136. Love Beyond | 183
137. Coming of Spring | 186
138. All Eternity | 187
139. Colors of Life | 187
140. Sacred Creed | 188
141. Seeking Pleasures | 188
142. Walk Softly | 189
143. True Self | 190
144. In Love | 193
145. Tangled Form | 195
146. Walk the Part | 196
147. Dust of Reality | 196
148. Autumn Breeze | 198
149. Morning Light | 198
150. Moving River | 199
151. Never-ending | 200
152. Beauty of Nature | 201
153. Soul of Nature | 205
154. Moon Flower | 206
155. Coming of Rain | 207
156. Moral Ground | 207
157. True Love | 208
158. All-Knowing | 208
159. Breath of Love | 211
160. Mosaic of Truth | 213
161. Oh, Lord | 216
162. Rustic Face | 217
163. Righteousness | 218
164. A Pebble of Reality | 218
165. Light of Wisdom | 219
166. Firm Ground | 219
167. Simple Life | 221
168. Mystified | 221
169. Web of Vanity | 222
170. Simplicity | 224
171. Being Human | 225
172. Conscious Moment | 227
173. Behind Time | 229
174. Touch of Love | 231
175. Awakened Mind | 233
176. Web of Dreams | 235
177. Wisdom in Truth | 238
178. Mystical Fragrance | 249
179. Birth of Spring | 249
180. Soul of Humanity | 250
181. Take Away | 251
182. Crying Laughter | 251
183. Guest for Life | 252
184. Moral Victory | 252
185. Wealth of Wisdom | 253
186. Nectar of Life | 254
187. Silent Words | 254
188. Water of Life | 255
189. Mirror of Truth | 255
190. Searching Eyes | 258
191. Heart of Giving | 258
192. Human Arrogance | 259
193. Endless Searching | 259
194. Life's Circle | 260
195. Wisdom of Insight | 260
196. Good of Humanity | 261
197. Will to Power | 262
198. Will to Conform | 262
199. Love Within | 263
200. Life's Center | 264
201. Whirling Dance | 264
202. Shallow Soul | 265
203. Walls of Time | 267
204. Blind Faith | 267
205. Human Pride | 268
206. Sacred Gift | 269
207. Human Banality | 269
208. Blind Greed | 270
209. Wish to See | 271
210. Water in Bowl | 271
211. Eyes Closed | 272
212. Time Lost | 272
213. Bridge to Reality | 273

Contents

214. Run Free | 273
215. Golden Rule | 274
216. Selfish Genes | 274
217. Hour to Toil | 275
218. Firm Ground | 275
219. Humble Submission | 276
220. Truthful ways | 276
221. Savage Nature | 277
222. Conscious Perception | 277
223. Spiritual Journey | 278
224. Walls of Silence | 279
225. Conscious River | 279
226. Oh, Solitude | 280
227. Deep Rooted | 280
228. Stillness of Life | 281
229. The Spirit Escapes | 282
230. Mocking Laughter | 282
231. Toward Salvation | 283
232. Withered Leaves | 283
233. One Moment | 284
234. Broken Seam | 285
235. Circle of Existence | 285
236. Veil of Life | 286
237. Wisdom in Truth | 288
238. I Am I | 299
239. The Climb | 302
240. Wealth | 302
241. Steps in Life | 303
242. Enter | 303
243. Soul of Spring | 304
244. Final Word | 305

Introduction

A POETIC IMAGINATION IS the wisdom of humanity which sheds light into the heart of darkness. It is the vision of beauty which our searching eyes long to see. Wisdom will become our moral voice which will guide us into our virtuous path toward salvation. True wisdom is ingrained in our footsteps as we walk through life to the end of time. We are bound by our essence to complete our spiritual journey with every breath of air that we take. Let There Be Wisdom In Truth was written in search of purpose and unity in our fragmented existence.

Our emotions drowned in reason give reality its artistic form. A poet's heart imbued with passion gives warmth and sweetness to nature's beauty. The spirit of poetry is written in words that will hold us sacred. The voice of conscious awareness is the moral fiber of our spiritual being. Mystical poetry is deeply rooted in human understanding and immersed in the mind of perception to become the light of human wisdom.

This second book of poetry was written under the weight of moral crisis in our world. Humanity at this moment in history is being challenged. The question of what it means to be human has become our moral dilemma. Does humanity have the courage for inner reflection and collective unity in consciousness? Poetry can heal the ailing spirit and gives strength to our humble character. Poetry can take away the darkness which blinds the soul and give us the truth in wisdom to strive toward righteous existence. Poetry can bring us together through our suffering. It can give us guidance in our moments of uncertainty. Poetry can give us a clear moral vision of truth and faith to overcome our differences and move toward the greater good.

Will humanity ever find the hidden path which will give it the essence of its being? Can we ever find harmony between mind, body, and soul which erases all boundaries between our inner and outer world? These questions are the essential features which this poetic work examines and

Introduction

seeks to answer. The soul of humanity clings to the fragile surface of time. We are at this moment in our history which will define the future of what mankind wills and what they hope to become. It is the spirit of poetry which can open our eyes to give courage and wisdom to remain steadfast in our human ways. Will you take my hand and walk through these verses, word by word, line by line, with every turn of page?

 Let wisdom be our guide to take us deep into our wondrous world. Will we ever overcome human ignorance which ties us in knots? What is this fate which holds us prisoner in our moral will? It is our well of needs which will not liberate the human spirit. Only wisdom of conscious awareness can set us free and humble us to live in our simple reality. Spiritual poetry is molded by our mystical mind and comes to the surface like water from the deep ocean. The seeds of experience hold all possibilities, but it is poetry which gives fruit to all that will come to be. Written with the breath of Sufism, these poems come to life with just one movement of the pen. A mystical poet writes no poetry, but only voices the love for divine wisdom. The vision to look deep into our existence is the light which will reflect the purity of wisdom in truth.

 No work ever comes to completion without the gracious and self-giving effort of individuals helping to bring it to its final form. In this time-consuming task, I asked for forgiveness from my family and friends for being too long absorbed in my work. I want to acknowledge the depth of my being to a very special person in my life. Prof. Dan Flickstein has been my teacher, my mentor, and my friend. His gift for teaching has been my vision, my wisdom, and my motivation for writing poetry. I have been humbled and honored that he critiqued and corrected my work. His constructive criticism and analysis gave the work its voice and substance. I am forever lucky to have a teacher who taught me the value of knowledge, love, and passion for serving humanity. I am also very grateful to Benjamin Aysan and Maliha Shakoor for their passion and artistic vision. Their illustrations gave life and power to my written words. I am very fortunate and forever grateful for their effort and enthusiasm. I owe them my deepest respect. They have been my drive and motivation to continue and complete this work of poetry.

 This book was written in good faith to my readers. I have been sincere in my words and I hope my sincerity does you no wrong, my readers. The words and vision in these poems come from a mediocre soul and I ask for your forgiveness first and last. I have found solace in my words and their

INTRODUCTION

virtue in moral simplicity has been my revelation into life. If wisdom is what it purports to teach, then I am at the mercy of what I have professed in these poems. A door into my conscious mind has been left open and I welcome all who wish to enter.

Root of Change

The season of change is upon our soul. The inward eye sees the ever-moving light reflected on the surface of time. Laughter will break through our silent moments, and the wind holds our spirit under the breath of conscious reality. Oh, spirit of being, will you erase the boundaries of existence and let us sleep through the night? Will everlasting dreams lessen the torments of our earthly moments? Can we ever overcome desires which give the heart their deepest pleasure? How can we tame our wildest emotions that will not humble to our human will? Humanity under the hand of progress can no longer accept the lessons of the past.

In moments of eternity, we are transformed, and conscious awareness is lost in vastness of time and space. It is our boundless form that holds true light of wisdom. Brush away the dust of simplicity and the complexity of life will bury us in layers of change. The mocking sound of laughter gives voice to our moral virtue of being human.

The metamorphosis of change is the hidden seed of reality. We are all rooted in our change; to grow beyond, we must not give it form. A journey through life is a thousand steps deep and begins with our first step. The mind compels us to write what the will has revealed, but words no longer obey our thoughts. The face of humanity is the vision of our truth. We gaze over the world sitting on a hill and reflect in silence the vision of our ever-changing awareness. The body will grow old with time; the spirit lurks in darkness, but the words of wisdom are never strange. Will we uproot our existence and open our eyes to the flickering light of change?

Winter's Bite

The all-consuming reality of winter holds humanity in deep slumber of dreams. The motionless trees frozen in their steps spread their branches to embrace the burden of nature. The bitter wind keeps the world strong-gripped, as the open landscape weights the gravity of winter's might. The ever white of winter's snow holds still human existence and traces their footsteps in time's etched journey.

Held in trembling fear we close our doors and hide in walls of comfort from the bitter cold of nature's fury. The coming of spring is nowhere to be seen. The colors of the world are no longer free, as the soul of winter holds them captive under its strong will.

Children still come out to play in their wintery playground. They heed no dread from winter's bite as their laughter warms their cheeks in the frosty chill. The human soul tumbles in snow, shivers in joy as they try to hit each other with hand-crafted snowballs. The sun filters its golden rays of light through dark gray clouds giving warmth to our shadowy world. The wind is on the move, howling, and in search of nature's loving form. Deeply rooted in the consciousness of existence is our humble awareness of winter's

spell. Will we take in the mist
of reality and breathe the
warmth of nature's beauty?

We find comfort in the walls of our
homes as we close our doors to
winter's unwelcomed arrival. On
dark winter nights, the moon looks
for the shades of nature's light and
the wind senses the fragrance of
spring. The parting steps of winter
are traced by the endless waves
of birds coming home, in pure
joyous rhythm of sound and
motion underneath
their wings.

Will of Body

A river moves silently with time and
whispers to the spirit to reflect on
its watered surface. Hidden reality
holds the mirrors of self-reflection
and won't let us see our true face. It
is the shadow in form that gives
light solace in our everlasting
existence. The human spirit will
walk toward the soul to erase the
vastness of infinite distance. A
spacious mind hungers for unity,
but it is the will of the body
which tears humanity apart.
What are we searching
for when the warmth
of the summer breeze
touches our hearts?

Eyes Opened

It was not until I opened my eyes that I began to see the world in all its wonders. Was the spirit not awoken when the wealth of the heart was plundered? Why become the target of envious eyes and put your life in danger? The wise have always told us not to open our doors to total strangers. It is the wealth in our health that sustains and holds life's great treasures. The greater your needs, the more time you waste chasing never fulfilling pleasures.

Being Born

A soul which bargains with time lives long night and day. The pleasures of the world are ours for the taking, but in want of more time, all turns to clay. We are born with our first cry into the world and grow up in sorrow of being born. Why do we live for love only to lose it with time which the heart comes to mourn? Time will give us no direction if the vision of reality holds us blind. If

we open our doors and
walk into ourselves,
then the joy of living
is what we will find.

Vanity

Oh, Vanity, you have made us
look at your world with no humanity.
Oh, Sanity, we have walked through
this world with all your insanity.
Oh, Morality, we are lost in darkness
without the wisdom of true reality.
Oh, Mortality, we die a thousand
deaths in rigid pride and calamity.
Oh, Hate, you have burned the soul
of humanity with your fiery
fate. Oh, Faith, you have revealed
the destiny of this world to
make us walk the path
of life straight.

Trapped in Doubt

A doubt that escapes the mind becomes the will of our moral character. The vision of imagination splits the unity of our reality. The fragments of conscious self become the residue of doubt in our existence. Layered in the dust of time we walk on our destined path, etched footsteps in life's will to be free. Why do we fear looking into the mirror of self-reflection? Are we afraid to see the true nature of our being? Is it the mocking laughter that we fear most? Is it the tears of joy or tears of sorrow that wash away the stains of human existence?

We have no time to doubt. The moments of our awareness are too constant, and the vision of our freedom is too clearly bound in light of wisdom. The heaviness of thought holds us under, but it is the simplicity of life that lifts the human spirit. Fear will run us in circles until we become faint in our steps and fall to the ground. A quiet life lived without examination will find no satisfaction in time. Like broken glass, it can hold no substance and unity of purpose. A doubt will trap us in our form and give the eyes no light to wash away the darkness. The beauty of children at play erases all doubts

in the moral wisdom of man.
Human virtue is lost when we lose
ourselves in the pleasures of worldly
existence. Tainted in doubt, we lose
the purity of our nature and
deny the human spirit
the vision of
its essence.

Let There Be Wisdom in Truth

The Forest Calls

The splendor of Nature will grow into our souls when we walk into the forest and free our spirit from the world. Will we forget our humanity once we touch the humble tree? The silent steps under our shallow existence will lighten the mind. The forest bears the sounds of our footsteps as the wind scatters the rustling leaves under our feet.

The night's mystery echoes with unknown danger, but our spirit grows bold with every sound of Nature's spiritual calling. The human spirit moves deep into the forest and becomes rooted in our imagination. The melody of music hums through the forest as the wind lifts the symphony of sound into the sky. The reality of existence becomes one with Nature and beauty of love erases all boundaries.

Under the great body of sacred mountains, a wolf howls into the night, beckoning the forest to find her lost love. A wise owl holds the vision of night, sitting on a trunk and reflecting the mystical moonlight in its eyes. The infinite sounds of the forest echo through the night, and the human spirit listens with open wonder. Youth becomes eternal and the world is forgotten as

we become one with the forest.
The forest is in full bloom at
dawn and the mist of night lifts
unhindered. The sun rises above the
horizon and the forest comes alive
with colors. The virgin beauty of
nature is no longer veiled from the
naked eye. Under the foothills
of mountains, humanity will
find the glory of Nature's
creation. Trees will lure us
in with their soft branched
fingers and life becomes
most beautiful when love
is purest. Will we breathe
in Nature's existence
and walk our spirit
into the deep-rooted
forest?

Human Greed

Drowned in the pleasure of
the world, the human spirit
becomes a slave to unsatisfied
needs. The complexity of life
deceives the soul and leaves the
spirit hollow like an unborn seed. We
long for love, but it is our selfish
desires which make the heart bleed.
In the will to be human, we have lost
the wisdom of our sacred creed.
Deeper than any ocean and stronger
than any emotion is our insatiable
appetite for flesh and greed.

Let There Be Wisdom in Truth

Why hoard wealth which burdens
our soul and will take
us to our end
with speed?

Hardship

The hardship of living will make us stronger and in the sanctity of life, we will not suffer. If we look at the world with open eyes, then the fear of suffering the heart will buffer. If we give ourselves to others, then our spirit will voice what our heart utters. A strong will can move with grace even when harsh reality becomes rougher. The human mind is the creative imagination that our spirit hides under. Those who overcome their fears and walk with an ironed will gain wisdom and with time become wiser.

Etched Emotions

The invisible hand of the wind awakens the senses to nature's joy with purity of deep devotion. Conscious awakening moves our spirit and touches our hearts with deep etched emotions. The thirst for fame is the deep nature of humanity which can't even drink a drop from this great ocean. A delicate flower naked to the world blossoms with beauty by the loving hands of creation. Nature's eye watches over the world and nourishes the soul with

nectar of salvation. Why
be afraid to walk on this
mystical journey which
can bring us closer
and closer to God's
revelation?

Total Freedom

Seeking true happiness is our
eternal thirst which is deeper
than any ocean. Will we walk into
our humble existence and bathe in
our heart's emotions? A journey
into our consciousness is vast;
opening our eyes to it becomes all-
encompassing. Will we open our
soul to the spirit within and savor
our existence with time passing?
Our light will reflect the
subtle shades of reality
which brings the mind infinite
wisdom. The joy of living
gives us the world as we
walk out of our door
into total freedom.

Entropy of Life

The night grows into twilight and pulls the veil over our dreams. If we are truly awake, then dreams and reality will become known only to consciousness. God's glory is revealed in light to those who look up toward the sky with silent wonder. Nature's colors are the essence of our vision which our eyes long to see. In the great abyss of eternity, we are but a speck of light which holds us in time. Our awareness drifts into reality as our mind holds us in our momentary existence. The hard boundaries of reality are carved by our perception to liberate our sculptured form. A mind weighs itself in heavy thoughts, but the spirit will unburden and offloads our thinking. The needs of life move our steps in many directions but we must pace them wisely.

We journey through time; the path of existence is pressed under our feet. A drop within a drop is like water within water which drowns our spiritual thirst. A mirror will reflect only reality, but our eyes will see it reversed. How deep is the ocean: the human mind is too shallow to realize. Before the dust settles on the surface of our consciousness, we must unearth the truth buried in our lies.

Let There Be Wisdom in Truth

The sands of time fall like raindrops
with every passing moment and in
the end, nothing will be left to fall.
The entropy of life spreads
into our consciousness
and everything that
comes into being will
break apart,
one and all.

Death and Life

Desires surrendered to the heart
no longer seek emotions that bring
humanity back into worldly pleasure.
Winter solstice is above and below
consciousness. The cold North wind
is the harsh reality, but a comfort to
the suffering soul. A selfless soul no
longer holds ground in human needs;
it is I in They and They in I that the
self cannot see. How mocking is the
laughter that burns our pride?
Oh, nature at the height of summer
solstice your desires lingers in
our spirit, voiceless, forever pure,
and virginal. Nature's beauty
holds us mystical between
the moonless night and
shimmering twilight.

Lost in the forest, the trees hold the
stillness of our dreams, and wait for
the day to open the doors to our reality.
It is our warm blood that bleeds with
emotions and spills on the surface of
mother earth. The consciousness of
our soul has not awakened and is
afraid to break through the surface of
our human form. The extremes of
our imagination cannot shoulder
the gravity of our heavy thoughts.
Will someone cut the wings of
freedom before they become lost
in the abyss of endless sorrow?

Etched in words, a mystical poet
brings to humanity the nature of
divine love. Wandering deep in the

forest, the trees comfort and hide her
from the dangers of becoming too
human. Housed under the glimmer
of her eyes is the light of God's
great wisdom. The beauty of simple
reality clings to her spirit as life
takes her into the soul of nature. She
seeks the divine and divine becomes
her seeking. Spiritual truth burns
deep in her soul and a mystical voice
escapes through her mind to
awaken her consciousness.

It is the hand of reality that
is unforgiving. It is love's
overwhelming emotion that
drowns the helpless soul. Like
rivers that merge with the great
ocean, the human spirit walks into
time to become the dust of life in
the vastness of space. Oh, what is
there to life, but to live and die for
desires that can never be fulfilled.
How deep is the well of our needs?
The thirst for eternity is the cup of
water that we no longer can drink.
Will humanity ever overcome its
imperfect existence? The passion
of living begins and ends with
each breath. If we desire the
world then it will be ours,
but we must first
bargain with life
and death.

Journey in Time

Under the light walks the shadow of our human form. Can we ever keep the calm within our storm? True wisdom will find harmony between two extremes and bring us back to our center. Will we let Nature become our sage to open the conscious eye and let the light of spirit to enter? Look at the world in silent wonder and what we will see is the body in soul. We all journey through time to live, act, and play our humble role.

Mind's Illusion

The night falls heavy upon our eyes as dreams drift through our conscious soul. Are we not a dream of mind's illusion or God's creative light in infinite whole? Human consciousness becomes blind when we cannot see true reality with eyes wide open. Will we ever listen to the sound of Nature through a poet's voice softly spoken? Are we not mind's

elusive reality which
blurs the lines of our
withered form? Will we
breathe in the calmness
of our existence and
walk calmly through
our worldly storm?

Unity of Self

The deeds of humanity hold no
virtue when it lives for pride in self-
righteousness. The fragments of
morality will remain broken until
we restore our humanness.
Like sediments in turbulent
water, we keep stirring the kettle.
Slow down your steps and be
patient with yourself and all
will settle. We have become
a mosaic of reality, searching
for vision in the unity of self.
Why search for truth in
all the wrong places
when it is already
within ourselves?

Dream World

A silent moment takes hold
of our mind and falls into our
conscious stream. Memories

shatter the stillness of time
and the conscious eye drifts
into our dreams. The world
is lost in sleep under the
warm residues of never-fading
twilight. The full face of the
moon comes out of the dark
clouds, glowing with warmth
of silver light. Will we ever
awake from our dreamy
world to become one with
time? Youth runs fast in
blood of humanity, but
it is aged wisdom
which is rustic
and sublime.

Conscious Stream

Time walks with our fate as we reflect on our journey through life. Every step will move us closer into our destined path. It is the curiosity of thought that moves the mind deep into the world. It is the perception of beauty that gives virtue to the creative soul of nature. The subtle motion of the wind will soothe our violent emotions which uproot our hearts. Will we open our senses to take in the miracle of life? Time falls upon consciousness like raindrops falling on the palms of our hands. Will we open our eyes to the light which travels through eternity and will come to rest in our soul?

A shadow will walk under our feet as we weather our existence with time. It is our humble will which holds us prisoner in our hearts. It is the fragrance of life which flowers spread into the festive breeze. It is the elation of our imagination which makes wisdom of knowledge so elusive. The more we seek, the less we seem to know. The more we try to hold on to knowledge the less intelligent we seem to become. There is nothing more revealing to the spirit than the truth of being human. True wisdom holds no boundaries and gives truth no form. If we free our minds from deep thoughts, then we will see

the true depth of their meaning.
Empires rise and fall when
they strive for greatness.

Humanity will mourn once they
embrace their heart with vanity
and power. The grandness of our
existence becomes great when we
let go of the pride in being human.
Life is drained by death when the
nature of our experience is squeezed
by the hands of oppression. Will we
walk in rhythm with life and find
harmony in our journey through
time? The beauty of nature rubs in
our eyes and the soul awakens us
in conscious light. Are we able
to hold our vision to the world? Are
we able to let go of our dreams to
live free from our human form? In-
stream of consciousness, the wind
holds our breath. The heart beats
faster and hungers for air
that it can't breathe.
Intelligence will
overcome pride
and wisdom
will humble
us in life
and death.

Silence

What is the nature of silence which echoes the voice of humanity into the valleys of time? The eyes of consciousness awaken the human spirit to remove the veil from our naked truth. Time is an endless stream which paves the road to take us far into the journey of life. It is our ever-moving footsteps which keep bringing us closer to time. There is great wonder in human eyes as the vision of reality is revealed once the fog of perception is lifted. Tears fall like raindrops as we absorb the emotions of existence which touches the heart of our human spirit. We hope to speak the written words of our fate, but worldly lips forbid them from being spoken. Silence will shatter our hard reality and the fragments of our existence will fall under our feet. We have become a mosaic of broken dreams that are no longer conscious of their spiritual wisdom.

The wind cuts into the edges of our form, sweeping through our past and spreading the dust of time that will settle into tomorrow. Silence becomes infinite and infinite becomes our silent moments. Why break the will of sound when we have become deaf to the voice of morality? Why do we still run toward freedom when we are still held captive in our caged will?

Let There Be Wisdom in Truth

Silence holds us empty when the words of our hearts are no longer real. The inner voice speaks to our soul; the secrets of our desires are no longer hidden. Can the mind move our body to act against the will of this world? Silence brews in our eyes; it takes hold of our vision. Words are caught in our tangled thoughts and reason erases all lines of certainty in mind's perception. Will silence unveil us from illusions of conscious living? How deep will wisdom fall as it twists and tumbles into our moral truth? Like a memory from our distant past, the echo of our story walks into the spirit fully conceived. Will we listen to the silent truth coming of age and listen to the wisdom that our soul conceived?

Etched

The world spins on its axis, round and round, unwilled and unhindered in time and space. It is our whirling spirit, round and round willed and hindered by the human race. Will we see the wholeness of our vision, which reflects our being through past, present, and future? The soul is torn with time, and the body bleeds with emotions,

yet only wisdom can heal and suture.
Etched in the footsteps of time,
all will come and go like ghosts
walking through narrow
winding streets. We are
caught in our conscious
trap and the spectacle
of life makes us puppets
in time complete.

Liberated

Vivid memories infused with
graceful colors cling to our youth
in smoldering moments of our
passing days. Oh, heart of burning
passion, you have ignited the flames
and there is no water to put out the
blaze. The wind wanders endlessly
searching for nature's fragrance
which is liberated and set free.
Will we take a moment to sit
under the mighty tree and feel
the tranquility which we don't
see? Silent memories move through
our past, trace the steps of life's
forgotten days. A journey
through consciousness
holds us in time,
no great or small
things ever stay.

Harmony

If truth is lost, then there
will be no human virtue,
only despair. Faith is born
into what we believe when
the human spirit embraces
piety in prayers. Those
who seek wisdom in simplicity
will nourish their mind with
peace and harmony. Be good
to yourself and the doors to
happiness will remain open
eternally. Divine wisdom
will guide our eyes to help
us through darkness. Will
we come out of our body
and soul with humility
to feel the touch of
God's holiness?

Wings

The will to seek knowledge is
never gained until we cast
it with simple wisdom. A caged
bird knows the burden of sorrow
when its wings are cut from
freedom. The web of consciousness
is spread wide by the mind of
humanity. The bait which sets the
trap is our hunger and desire for
vanity. Truth holds us prisoner
when the heart can't escape
the lure of love. The hands

Let There Be Wisdom in Truth

of reality open into the
sky and there flies
the soulful dove.

Let There Be Wisdom in Truth

Silent Reflection

Will we burn away our paper
existence, tear away the pages
of time to let go of our words
that plague our soul? We bring
ourselves into the world to hold love
for humanity in our spirit. Will we
give up the need for freedom which
brings no peace and harmony? Truth
can never liberate our mind when
we become prisoners in a world
of seeking. Will we let our
emotions break the heart which
no longer can hold true love?

Let the spirit walk free to breathe in
the fragrance of nature's mystery. If
the soul remains in darkness, then
what will our eyes see in truth
of human wisdom? A candle's
eye becomes elusive when
it sheds tears of wasted
time. A shadow which
lingers in our form has
escaped into the
light of our dreams.

The wings of reality lift
our thoughts as curiosity
takes flight into the vast of our
imagination. Why not surrender
our will to the beauty of being?
What becomes of suffering which
sorrow can't wash away with
tears? The road toward life
is never straight, but we must
journey on to come back home
someday. Time moves beneath

our feet and written in stone is
our weather-beaten age. In silent
reflection, we search for direction
as memories trace the path of life's
steps back to our beginning. Why
burn the forest which will turn the
spirit to ashes? Human passion
will enflame the mind and the
embers of our emotions will
consume the body whole.

In the smoldering and swirling
smoke of reflection, time will
spread us far and wide until
we are no more. Etched
in our moments are the
reminiscences of our once
youthful form framed
in our timeless reality.
Have we become too human
and no longer can live in the
wisdom of truth? Why not
burn away our lingering
vision in time past?
Our will to live is
consumed in our earthly
dreams and the mold
of our existence has
hardened at last.

Spirit in Form

Humanity will grow in its human nature and come of age in reality fully formed. Is it the fate of our existence that holds us on shallow ground? Pressed under the pages of time are the words of humanity that tell the story of our conscious being. The essence of life is written in our emotional history. The humble soul will bring them into our conscious mind. In the depth of time, the human spirit keeps still, as the will to move makes the body restless. The steps of humanity are heavy with doubt as they journey through time opened at both ends. Human nature will feast on the flesh of reality, ravenous, ever so hungry to devour wealth, pride, and fame.

Our senses have become drunk on the sweet honey nectar of nature's seductive charm. The veil of perception has been lifted and the light of truth awakens the eye toward wisdom. The lines of sanity are blurred by fast-moving thoughts, flickering through the stillness of our mind's eye. Plagued by spiritual decay we acquire the musty odor of truth in being human. Human lust for wealth is blind lunacy; morality withers and dies in the hands of vanity.

The moral fabric of our existence burns in emotions of hate. We cut our heads and stain our hands with the blood of humanity. Fish live in rivers and are never thirsty for their water. Man lives for great wealth and treasures of the world but always thirsts for more. Does he not know that all that he seeks is within and nowhere else in the world? What is certain, the blind man will only touch the walls of darkness. In the roots of our soul, the body does not exist. The spirit lays dormant, ready to be awakened only when we give in to the voice of wisdom. What will become of humanity when time erases all traces of its existence?

Consciousness etched in human form, no words are spoken, and no reflection reflects the light of its essence. It is our savage nature, self-destructive, and self-conceived that holds no salvation for life of existence. Are we the inspiration for God's great love of creation? It is human awareness that sees into darkness, but the light of wisdom blinds the eyes that seek too much understanding. How far we have gone into the world and yet we still can't find our true home. If we could liberate our spiritual form from our body of needs, then the light will cast no shadow. How deep we crave for the world which leaves

Let There Be Wisdom in Truth

the spirit naked and no place to
hide. Time will carve our
raw nature and the soul
will liberate us from
human pride.

Curiosity

The axis of our soul is rooted in
the spokes of reality and keeps
our life spinning. The richness
of treasures can be lost in one
moment, but no one can take
away our wealth in learning.
Built on curiosity, the sediments
of knowledge settle into the
depth of our imagination.
The more we know, the less
we will grow if pride
holds our mind's creation.
If we seek to know that
which cannot be known
then our curiosity will
go round and round in
endless circles. The
measure of intelligence
is our human ignorance
and life's final
hurdle.

Limits

The truth will escape through
our veiled reality and become
the moral wings of freedom.
Knowledge will open our eyes
and curiosity will seep through
the light of wisdom. We are like
distant stars, a flickering light in
vastness of space. Will humanity
ever come to terms with its human

nature which hides behind its masked face? Intelligence is measured through our limitations. How can we reach infinite time with our humble imagination?

Fool in Folly

Humans flaunt their knowledge with pride and wag their tail for praise in folly. The walls of knowledge build the story of humanity with an ironic twist of melancholy. Civilization lives in their world of dreams and spends their lives lavishly in time borrowed. The body is our only home, the spirit will hold it with sorrow. The miracle of insight gave humanity the power to rule. Savage remains human nature, and with time becomes more condescending than the all-knowing fool.

Frozen

The howling cold wind blows
through the winter snow and sends a
shiver down the spine of our will.
Ever-white landscape glazed by
nature's hand leaves the
strong trees frozen in winter's
great chill. Humanity shelters from
harsh reality in the warmth of its
home. Winter's strong grip holds us
deep in the marrow of our bones.
The sun fades from the sky and the
clouds darken their mood. The
soul of nature sleeps in
solitude until the harsh
winter's night
is subdued.

Freed Spirit

Wings of freedom broken by the self-willed hands of humanity are held captive by the spirit of time. In the winding road of self-perception, consciousness awakens in the deep stillness of reality. The wind is spontaneous and wanders free, ever-moving with grace through the world to touch the sleeping soul. Can we ever hold our existence against time? The voice of nature will echo our mystical moments in time as we come of age.

The web we weave is our mind's own tangled fate. We become imprisoned in our bodies, and the spirit holds captive the sacred soul, both waiting to be liberated. Like a caged bird, we sing, as the voice of hope infuses suffering into our song. Will we breathe in the world and breathe out our human substance? If we listen to our wisdom, it will become the rhythm of sound, subdued under our breath. Why not become a forest of banyan trees, rooted toward the sky, and growing into the womb of mother earth? Will we ever erase the lines between high and low, rich and poor, and between man and woman? Our spirit is like water that burns the ocean, setting ablaze to passions which leave no water to burn. Are we a dream reflected in illusions or an illusion reflected

in dreams? Will we have the courage
to give up freedom to buy back our
souls? Will we swallow the spirit
whole and wash it down with the blood
of humanity? A mind is freed
to think once the hunger for
knowledge is fulfilled. The beauty
of nature will grow evermore even
when humans will to destroy. What
takes away free will is the freedom
which we give away without truly
being free. To live is to die for
freedom and to die is to live for
freedom. We are born to move
toward our end, but in dreams,
we try to erase every beginning
moment of our existence.

It is the will to move that cuts us free
from our tangled existence. Why
become a slave to blind rituals when
God's faith has no home. Will we
learn to close our eyes to see our
inner world? Will we learn to chase
the wind and not be tempted to hold
it in our hands? Will we learn to
breathe underwater and not drown in
our thirst? Will we free our spirit
from human needs and take the two
ends of life and tie them into a knot?
The sun's rays dip deep on the
horizon and the light dims our
conscious awareness. The mind
reflects silently into the sunset as
humanity sleeps into the night.
The human spirit opens
its conscious doors and
looks to the sky and
takes flight.

Move with Time

All things will move with time. Life is a journey which will walk toward infinite reality. The moment of realization settles in our conscious mind, but we remain sleeping with eyes wide open. We are given one life but go through many deaths. It is the pride of human nature to deny its mortality. Like lotus leaves that live on the surface of water, we live on the surface of our dreams.

Heavy are the footsteps of humanity as they walk on the road toward life's long journey. Time will bring us to wisdom; there is no wisdom gained when lies are hidden in truth and truth lays hidden in lies. We are bound to ourselves, like rooted trees bound to earth. A stagnant soul is blind to the vision of light and cannot see beyond itself. If we doubt our existence, then there will be no reasoning with our perception of time. If we move our mind, hold the body still then the world will move all around us. Walk with time, be spontaneous in life's moments, and come toward the center of your being with ease of mind. If we open our eyes and look into ourselves then the mystical purpose of existence is what we will find.

Let There Be Wisdom in Truth

Beauty of Nature

The road toward nature is winding, twisting, and turning with every move and step we take. The sun sinks into the horizon, light paints the sky with an infinite hue of colors. Open fields stretch into the great distance and our vision is transformed by nature's splendor and mystical form.

The mighty rivers glimmer, moves in seamless, wavy motion, which touches the mind of human wonder. The virgin beauty of nature rests on red loving roses drenched in morning dewdrops. Oh nature, you grow into the heart of a mystical poet whose vision in words flow with passion with no will to stop.

Mystical

Cloud cover veils the warm ivory glow of the full-faced moon. A lover's eyes reflect the seductive passions of the night as the wind chants nature's mystical tune. Will we listen to the music

which gives us the melody
of nature's love? Look
out the window; the soul
of the night is hovering
below and above. The stars
sparkling glory watches
over the world as twilight
takes us deep into our
dreams. The majesty of
lucid reality will journey
through our imagination
to take our emotions
to the extreme.

Aged Wisdom

The coldness of humanity numbs the
human spirit. The charms of nature's
beauty become an idle dream. A
heart's inner storm becomes the
calm of our center. We are deeply
rooted in our human fate and only
love can bring us the light of eternal
bliss. Memories pressed in our
vision ferment with age and bring
moments to the surface from
forgotten time. Slow-moving rivers
that run through our dreams seek
union with our conscious ocean. The
face of humanity reflects aged
wisdom, layered in sediments of
morality, set heavy and deep. Life
into death, we journey through
time; a moment of conscious
awareness is all that
we can keep.

Human Mold

The light of consciousness will
reflect on the surface of reality.
A reflective mind molds us into our
human form and gives us the face of
individuality. The human spirit hides
under the shadow of our existence,
where the light of wisdom is sublime
and warm. The soul of humanity
has touched the heart to
calms the spiritual storm.
Will we ever become aware
of our moments in time
given? The treasures of
the world are not for
keeping but a glimpse
of what is in
heaven.

Perception

It is deception, pure deception which
made us believe in the delusions of
our perception. It was perception,
pure perception which made us
believe in the deception of our
reflection. It was affection, deep
affection which blankets our naked
body with warmth of affection. It
was objection, true objection which
gave us the courage to hold the
world under our moral objection.
The mirrors of our soul reflect
the light of the world, pure

reflection which displays the
faults of our perfection.
It was a strong conception
of our will truly conceived
which will bring our
being into conception.

A Guest Within

A guest walks through our door, invisible to the eye, but tender to the soul. Like branches of a loving tree, which welcome birds home; we embrace our guests with our hearts. A guest is a heavenly light which reflects through the windows of our eyes. Love for humanity is open-ended and becomes the sacred truth of God's wisdom. A guest will warm the spirit and break all barriers to human love.

The footsteps of humanity are moving toward us and calling our name. Will we open our hearts, our doors to the one who longs to come in? Does the guest reside within or do we reside within our guest? The world of reality is lost in raindrops, lost in the depth of our ocean. We are a guest of this world and the guest becomes our world. A guest is a hidden treasure that we do not see; we are seeking and searching for them in all the wrong places. A guest is here today and will forever remain a blessed moment that our heart embraces.

Oh, Children

Oh, children of this world you bring harmony and color to the soul of humanity. Wisdom grows through the sounds of laughter and spreads with splendor into the wind. The beauty of simplicity is clear to the mind as nature becomes the spirit of love. Let us not lose the child within as we grow old and worldly. Porous is the vision of reality as the eyes of children become the deep well of truth under the open sky. A child is I; thou art the man, there is only light which holds us pure in our human form. Sweet as the summer breeze which touches our senses, children will purify the spirit of humanity. Like the majestic sun, children warm the heart and give purpose to our humble existence.

Oh, children of this world, you are the delicate flower of God's conception. Will you spread your fragrance into the heart of man's cold nature? You are a gift to the world, a treasure to the human race. The simplicity of life and the virtue of happiness can be ours if we follow your role. Oh, children of this world, man is the great substance and you are the water that fills his bowl.

Let There Be Wisdom in Truth

Fair Wind

A fair wind moves through the open fields and spreads the transcendent fragrance of nature's soul. Trees stand proud and strong in their humble stance; motionless, ever so still, as leaves flicker, flutter, and drift in the wind. An image of heaven opens into the forest, virtuous and divine. The symphony of sound is elusive and spills into the air by the unseen body of the gentle breeze. It is the splendor and artistic work of nature that liberates the vision of earthly beauty. The moon's ever watchful eye never sleeps, as the soul of night bathes in the warmth of ivory glow.

Mountains in their jagged peaks shoulder clouds as snow gives way to icy rivers. The cold-water slips, tumbles, and moves toward the foothills; racing through the sloped landscape to meet the great ocean. Birds sail under their wings; sheer is their will to overcome and lift over high mountain cliffs. A gust of wind wails down the high hills and hums through the meadow in ghost like chants. The North wind moves south, carving into the canvas of cold tundra, and melts away the frozen footsteps of nature's path. The power of the wind scatters the dusty snow and lifts the earthly cover from the surface of time.

Let There Be Wisdom in Truth

Oh, wind what is in your will
that makes you move? What do
you become when you come to a
standstill? We breathe you into our
existence and breathe you out into
the world. You have become
a secret of nature's most sacred
mystery. With great joy, humanity
will chase, and hold you against your
will, but you leave them behind with
no great regret. Oh fair wind, how
vast is your reach and how deep you
permeate into our consciousness!
You move with grace, and in the
heart of this world, you
embrace all, selfless
and in love, remains
anonymous.

No Holding Time

Time fades into eternity and the passing moments become eternal, timeless, and cling to our human experience. Lingering in our withered souls are the forgotten memories of rustic time. Sweetness of life is the sweet honey of nature which infuses our hearts with color and beauty. A touch of light burns the senses, and we become the ashes of our loving form. We have become a forest of dreams rooted into our imagination. Are we to become the tree in our forest or the forest with no trees? So much silence begs for solitude that we remain silent under the stillness of time. We search for words with meaning and purpose in our moving and changing thoughts. How do we voice the truth which has become deaf to our ears?

The coming of age holds our feet to the ground as we run through youth with fast-paced steps. We lose our desire for the world as we come nearer to the end of life's journey. Why do we keep our eyes open when we have closed our vision for wisdom and truth? In the fields of deep emotions, children come to play in our nightly dreams. Awakened by the warm glow of light, we look out our window and children no longer play their worldly games. Time heavies our steps toward life and our joints will

ache and grind to a halt. We
live between the boundaries of
reality and our beginning and end
finally come back to our center.

The days and nights of our lives are
layered with sentiments and lined in
our faces. The human spirit searches
for its reflection in the mirror of
translucent time. The mind will
voice its conscious existence to those
who wish to hear. We humble our
self to simplicity as wisdom ripens
with age. Eternity of time is etched
in every stone. Life will start to
wither and decay the moment it is
born. The needs of the world leave
us empty; the pleasures of life give
us grief. There is nothing worth
keeping when time will come and
take us away. The more we gain the
less we can hold. Time judges all
with singularity of purpose.

Time holds no distinction between
rich or poor, great or small, and
between life or death. Every
moment of existence is infinite
in life's collective treasures.
Time is all-encompassing and
all-consuming. Can we ever
hold time in our hands? We
are a grain of dust in time,
pressed in the shifting
lines of sand.

Neglect

When a tree falls in the forest,
no one hears it but the ground.
Words that fall on deaf ears
speak loudly but make no sound.
How great is our thirst for
worldly pleasures that we become
slaves to it with our spirit bound?
Why do we burden the body with
gluttony of needs and keep gaining
weight, pound after pound? Time
will hold us in a circle, never
coming back to us when it
turns around. If we hide
from the truth then in
our lies, we will
surely be found.

Law and Justice

Laws which are unbending and
oppressive often will not be
followed. The poor are forced to take
in the decrees, but the rich will find
them hard to swallow. The hands of
justice which uphold the moral truth
quell the savage and evil side of
human nature. There is no greater
destructive force in our world than
humanity when it becomes a blind
greedy creature. A civilization
which is oppressed by a few
will have no air to breathe
in freedom. Power will

corrupt human nature
only when the mind
is weak in strength
of reason.

Leadership

A true leader finds fault in herself for things that go wrong and gives credit to others for what goes right. A leader holds wisdom when she remains calm in turmoil and holds firm with conviction and might. It is empathy and compassion which will win the hearts of millions. Humility will wash away the pride of human nature and make our moral judgments more resilient. To move the masses with great passion, one must guide them with clarity of goal. Once the human spirit breaks through the walls of stagnation, then a nation can no longer hold prisoner the mighty soul.

Yet So Near

The eyes of reality are closed
to the world, and yet the vision
of truth has remained so clear.
A life journey is pressed under our
footsteps and the distance seems so
far and yet so near. Dear God, were
we not born to spread the truth of
man? We will keep wasting
moments in eternity, destroying
our spirit in one single lifespan.
How far will we search for the truth
in a world which keeps spinning
in a never-ending dance? The
circus of life is the fate of
humanity, a drama
in human folly with
an ever-mocking
glance.

Wisdom in Sorrow

A prisoner of will we become and suffering in humanity we can't overcome. Dear Lord, heal thy spirit, cut away the disease of pride, and give the world the compassion of your wisdom. How will we know the I in You or the You in I when the soul is blind to both? It is pain in suffering we wish to avoid, but it is suffering in pain that comes to destroy. Human nature is humbled by grief and the spirit grows strong by living through sorrow. Suffering will twist humanity in knots, and emotions will swirl in their hearts like burning embers in smoke. How do we overcome and escape life in our body of sorrow?

Why not bring joy into sorrow like light into darkness? It is only through suffering can we come to know the true worth of happiness. Will we listen to the wisdom of the Vedas, Quran's musical poetry, and Bible's love of human virtue? We are all one mosaic in many fragments of reality. The mind, body and spirit will become free from suffering once we let go of our humanity in times of spiritual crisis. Let us burn to ashes the needs of the world; quench our thirst with purity of water. Let us breathe in and out of life's existence and give time no moments in suffering. It is our consciousness of collective suffering that will give salvation to humanity. The light of hope keeps us warm in our cold world of reality. Water which holds our thirst can no longer fill our cup. Darkness which fills our hearts with fear will not give us courage in wisdom. It is the nature of two extremes that brings us back to the center of our being. The pendulum of life swings back and forth between happiness and sorrow; where it will stop depends on who holds the strings of our fated existence. Will we awaken our soul to see us move through life and death in one pass of time?

Can we see our reflection in our bowl of water? Will we give our body the power to overcome the pangs of hunger? Will we give our perception the power to overcome reality? Will we give our soul the power to overcome the spirit of being human? Will we give ourselves the sorrow of others with our outstretched hands? Will we give ourselves the courage and strength to break through the strong walls of sorrow? Will we shed no bitter tears that suffering brings to our spirit? Will we ever fall in love again as at this moment, our heart seems forever broken?

Let There Be Wisdom in Truth

We will grow deep roots in
conscious reality to spread out
into the world. We must live
through all emotions of the world to
become truly human. The rise
of civilization has touched all
corners of the world, but human
nature still has not overcome its
savagery and banality. To
become human, fully human,
we must see the wisdom
in suffering and seek
truth in morality.

Let There Be Wisdom in Truth

Mystical Embrace

How do we reconcile with the power of our human nature? We move in and out of our ghostly existence, trapped in our form, only to be liberated by the light of wisdom. The wind moves to awaken the sleeping soul. What is this mystical laughter that echoes through our meditative mind? Motionless, we sit as our eyes look deep into life seeking the purpose of our existence. We trace the path of wandering clouds to eye the path of life's worldly journey. We gaze at the strong, tall standing trees and see our footsteps rooted in time. We are enriched by the beauty of nature and try to embrace the miracle of being human.

It is the bitter winter that moves us deep into our walls of comfort. The scent of spring awakens our spirit to the colors of the world. The warm summer breeze brings music of nature's love into our hearts. Will we lift the veil from our consciousness and let nature touch our human soul? Memories filter time and become the sediments of reality that fall into our outreaching hands. The mold of our existence changes with Nature's mood as we bathe in the purity of human emotions. Life will fall in love with time as we surrender our will to the night. The moon burns bright with sensuous, seductive shades of silver-gray light which holds all in its mystical embrace.

Dewdrops cling to humble leaves and reflect their darkened pearly glow under the dimness of moonlight. Twilight drowns the shallow rivers and moves toward the horizon in a harmonious glow. Dawn awakens and spills the red-purple haze of the sun onto the dome of the morning sky. Singing birds break the silence of time and the wind goes into its whirling, dust-filled dance. The glory of light erases darkness and brings out the infinite colors of nature's beauty. Endless yearning holds us in our moments as we become enchanted in our heart's emotional storm.

Nature watches over her mystical world and finds no comfort in the cold bitterness of winter. Dark, subdued, slow-moving clouds walk over the sky in never-ending pilgrimage across the earth. Humanity runs toward the warmth of life's existence but can't find any solace in living. Human nature has become bittersweet and takes great pleasure in the ripe reality of being human. Flushed faces, red-rose cheeks take cover as winter's charm stirs the wind. The ascent of the splendid sun breaks the will of reality and brings life into nature's vast kingdom.

Oh, humble spirit we hold our
bodies warm in winter coats as
we walk quicker, and the blood
moves deeper into our hearts.
The changing moods of reality
are deep-rooted in the seasons which
time brings. We look through our
windows as the world looks into our
souls. The heart of nature will warm
our spirit. The rivers of life will thaw
and move freely under the frozen
earth. We look to the sky in
search of homecoming
birds and marvel at
nature's rebirth.

Hard Reality

Between life and death there
is only consciousness, as
between light and darkness,
there is only hard reality. Our
search for truth lies within
ourselves and our depth of
moral character flows through
human morality. What is it that
we are seeking which takes us far into
our winding road? It is our human
pride which moves us from
our center and swings heavily
the pendulum of our spiritual
load. Can we know the wisdom
which light brings into our
hearts? The goal of the
wicked is to spread fear and

shatter the wholeness
of truth into
fragmented
parts.

Lost Path

If we run away from the world
to hide in our lies, then we will
find no comfort in our truth.
Why burden consciousness
with our humanity and give
morality no wisdom to awaken
in youth? The guilt of humanity
seeps into our consciousness
as we take a moment to correct
our wrongs. Moral goodness
can never be lost if we keep it
close to our hearts where it
belongs. Wandering blind, we
lose our ways and the road to
our journey no longer holds our
feet. A path through righteous
living eases our mind and
brings music to the
world that is soulful
and sweet.

Just Look

Hypocrisy! Hypocrisy! Hypocrisy!
Just look into the mirror
and you will see. The truth will
unmask our lies and naked in
consciousness we shall be. Oh,
mindful soul, how blind has
humanity become that they
can't even see their mortality?
Dear Lord, why do you
remain silent when humans

shed the blood of your morality?
Hypocrite! Hypocrite! Hypocrite!
Just look into yourself and you
will agree. How far from
the truth we have strayed
and how quick
from moral
consciousness
we flee.

Life and Death

The night falls heavy on our breath.
Darkness is born through life and
death. These eyes have seen reality
in sordid dreams. Night falls on
our surface like a pebble upon a
conscious stream. Emotions move
like waves seeking to touch our
loving souls. Light awakens
our eyes and searches
for unity in our
fragmented
whole.

Conscious Veil

The power of imagination will
shatter the glass reality of our mind
to take flight into infinite wonder.
It is love of life which we
seek in nature's beauty which

Let There Be Wisdom in Truth

the heart longs to plunder.
The veil of our conscious
eyes have been lifted and
the soul awakens in a state
of ecstasy. Like a wandering
mystic, the human spirit
rejoices and dances in
its spiritual melody.
Will we become mindful
of our moments in living
and sit down with time and
enjoy the glorious breeze?
Oh wind, you walk with
such humble pride; will
you let us breathe
you in, please?

Drifting in Time

The face of humanity holds no light until it opens its eyes to the beauty of nature. We smell the fragrance of life and breathe in the serenity of conscious existence. Deep in the emotions of our heart, we say the words which give our mind solace in simple thoughts. We are the shimmering light in the divine glory of our youth. We are the mystical vision which fades into the distance but emanates from our inner eye. The footsteps of humanity are fixed and pressed in time. The wisdom of age holds no hour but carries our conscious burden throughout the day. The colors of nature glow in conscious perception in our mindful eye.

Will we open our hearts and let love reflect in our souls? We race to catch the floating leaf that drifts in the wind and settles in our imagined existence. We are all drifting in time, trying to catch ourselves in moments of drifting. Oh nature, forgive the human soul which looks at you with blind eyes. Oh nature, your beauty is eternal. We are but a stain in the purity of your form. Oh nature, you come into the soul with silent steps and awaken us from our deep slumber. Will we quench our thirst with sweetened dewdrops which cling to the petals of maiden flowers? A

vision of inspiration escapes the
mind, like flaming and colorful
butterflies taking flight toward
the glorious blue sky.

The wind moves with a unity of
purpose and touches the world with
a softness of serenity. Dreams echo
through time and tinkle with laughter
of children at play. Human emotions
conscious of their deep love embrace
the world with their loving arms. We
have become a vision of nature's
beauty which molds our existence
and gives reverence to the soul of
creation. Oh, fair wind, will you
breathe life into our spirit and
walk into our consciousness?
Nature's mystical world
blossoms with time and
waters the seeds of
our awareness.

Joy in Sorrow

Held in human sorrow is our mind's
infinite need for self-realization.
What will rise from mother earth is
the mystical nature in the oneness of
love. The taste for life is the sweet
fruit of God's great love for
humanity. The human spirit is lost
in illusions of Self and has become
too opaque in its human form.

Time never holds still, human
emotions will run in circles; the
wind takes hold and dilutes the
fragrance of our existence. It is joy
in sorrow that becomes our comfort in
the warm summer breeze. Our eyes
remain open, but we have closed our
hearts to simple beauty. Will we
take a moment to pause and watch
children at play? Will we look at the
light of conscious reflection and
wash away our human form?
Nurtured in our mother's womb
we come out into the world, crying.
We are guests in this world,
our sorrow is infinite, but
joy is our moments
for living.

Autumn Leaves

Spring breaks into autumn; birds
bid it farewell as heartbroken

trees give it a rustic ginger-brown look. Withered leaves broken by the strong hand of the wind are scattered in their last moments of life which autumn took. A rose naked to the world shows love's true colors, but to the envious eyes of humanity gets plucked too soon. The cold autumn breezes run through the night, as river's stillness reflects the silver-gray of the shimmering moon. Sprinkled here and there are the dying memories of flowers that autumn collects. Spring sees the taking of nature's beauty and mourns leaving with great regret.

Conscious Love

Divine is love of nature. A mystic poet dances in the oneness of love like a dervish dancer. Mystery of life is filled with wonder, there are more questions than answers. The words of wisdom wandered into her mind and whispered the secret of existence that willed her to be. What is life but a poetic vision that waits for her conscious eye to see.

Let There Be Wisdom in Truth

Nature of Man

The spirit of humanity moves through conscious existence and comes into reality unchanged. The history of man's nature is the story of a never-ending thirst for greatness and power. In a world which is sacred and pure, man will pollute it with vanity and pride. Will man ever walk into wisdom and find the truth in simple living? If he takes in too much life, then he will overwhelm and drown his spirit. True purpose for existence is to take time and reflect on the purpose for living. A journey through life is to walk with our feet and unburden the soul from worldly lures. A noble soul is never tangled by life's never-ending needs and walks free unburdened.

The wealth of man's spirit is to take in less, not more. Eyes which open into light can no longer hide the darkness in man's heart. Man becomes whole when the perception of reality becomes the perception of his will. The shadows of our dreams erase the boundaries of reality once we lose ourselves in sleep. We bow our heads low to the divine, but what we see in the divine is the image of ourselves.

How profound is human passion and how grand is their will to be? When time is most ripened, we sell ourselves short. Oh, withered leaves, we hold tomorrow in our hands today. We are born into our beginning and move toward our end; there is no end to our beginning. The road through our existence is bound to our feet. It is the needs of our body which hold the mind empty in thoughts. Is freedom what moves man's spirit or is freedom ever free to move unwilled? We are the broken fragments in the unfinished mosaic of our imperfect whole. We are born through the existence of nothingness and through it, we come into existence. The way of the world is the heart of life and the root of our suffering. When a man can't find his way, then life will not give him a way into the world. The oneness of reality is one with him only when the mind, body, and spirit bring him to unity.

True perfection is realized when man humbles his pride at the feet of his imperfection. The shadow of his form is the form in his shadow, only when light embraces his real spirit. The only way a man can gain his true self is to sell it to the lowest bidder. Life will hold us in our water. Man is like a thirsty river from which no one can drink. A life spent chasing the wind is like achieving greatness after one's death. Can man breathe in and breathe out his

humanity with
the same
breath?

Chasing Humanity

The power of will fulfills our duties and opens our hearts to the great light of truth. The wisdom of the world holds time still in the great splendor of youth. Why live in empty dreams which will not open our eyes to a world of possibilities. Will humanity ever awaken from its fantasy of eternal living in time infinite? We are born in simplicity but get caught in the web of complexity. Will we ever free ourselves and move toward the humble ways of humanity?

Mask of Deception

In the soft glow of twilight, the universe holds us in the vastness of its existence. Life is not measured in time, but in courage to walk the distance. How did we come to be and who will show us the wisdom to walk in the right direction? Only through the light of morality can we realize the birth of our inception. In a world of delusions even when we hit the wall of reality, we still deny its perception. When will we become conscious of reality and unveil the mask of deception?

LET THERE BE WISDOM IN TRUTH

Voice of Wisdom

It was only in our loving thoughts
that the mind was caught by surprise.
The spirit was elevated, and
awareness came into being with
wide-opened eyes. The vision
of reality filters through our
consciousness and never dies.
Humanity can move no
further until it walks
away from its lies. Who
knows the voice of wisdom
which spoke of reason to
the wise? It is to be human,
only human and
pride will lead to
our demise.

Moral Gaze

Words have grown deep roots in the
soul of our life's story. There is only
shame for the naked body when
clothed in human glory. Vivid
moments in colors of time
are but smoldering moments in
life's passing days. The blood
of humanity runs deep in our
emotions, like water bound to clay.
We are born into our conscious eyes
to live in our human ways. Will
we ever come to terms
with humanity, and lift the
mist of the world with
our moral gaze?

Mystical Love

It is her mystical eyes which gave poets the vision to write. The heart is captured by her beauty and eyes bring her to sight. She has become a lover's dream and glows warm in a candle's light. The moonlight casts her shadow as stars open their soul to the darkness of night. Love can hold no form until her face is freed by the divine hands of creation. She has touched the soul and the awakened spirit is our pure salvation.

Moral Truth

We long to lift the veil of truth and yet it is our human nature that blinds us to all understanding. The nakedness of truth reveals all and holds no shame under the eyes of moral virtue. Words which hold simple wisdom never fail to be realized. The spirit of righteousness is the heart of moral truth. The face of human virtue can never be forgotten once consciousness carves our human mold. Nature holds the light of creation and becomes the beacon of our soul. Pride consumed by human passions cloud us to the wisdom of clear reason. Human nature drenched in jealousy becomes trapped in their web of emotions. The spirit of a just society can never come together until collective consciousness seeks unity in its moral character. The human spirit that goes blind, runs into many dead-ends of certainty, with eyes wide open.

It is the light of wisdom reflected in our faces that we wish to see. It is our raw fury that cuts our emotions and makes us bleed. What is known cannot be erased and what is erased cannot be known. We are born into our spiritual form, molded by the will of experience, and hardened by the lessons of reality. Are we the mud in our water or the water in our mud? Truth will fragment with time

and guilt of conscious morality will
have to collect the broken pieces.
Only human awareness will hold us
in our moments and bring unity to
our existence. Like flickering lights
in the universe, the truth fluctuates
within our reflective gaze. Truth
folds on itself like moments
folding on moments by the
loving hands of divine will.
How do we loosen the knots
of worldly needs and nourish
the soul with simple wisdom?

How will we know the truth when
we bury ourselves in worldly lies?
Truth will free the soul and the mind
will walk into the house of reason.
Truth in beauty is the beauty we seek
in truth. The eternal truth is the
basis of our moral being. Truth will
reflect in our eyes the mirror of self-
reflection and self-reflection will
become the moral light in our
reflection. The spirit of wisdom
is the truth of humanity

Do we have the courage to speak the
moral truth and defend it against the
world of hypocrisy? Truth upholds
the ideals of wisdom; truth gives us
liberty to free the mind; truth lives in
justice and justice is the fabric of our
humanity. It is the intrinsic nature of
Self that escapes our awareness.
Truth moves like the wind, invisible,
serene, and bends with ever-
changing reality. It is the words in

Let There Be Wisdom in Truth

wisdom that makes us human and it
is wisdom in our words that
makes us humane. The birth of
consciousness is the moral vision in
our eyes. Moral virtue is the breath
for life and in truth, it lives
and in truth, it
never dies.

Web of Darkness

Oh, Kabir, will we ever see the web of darkness that lies within our eyes? The trap is set for our emotions as we bear our soul to the will of humanity. Will we let our spirit wander over towering mountains where imaginations know no bounds? Oh, Kabir, time flows like rivers in our existence and the soul no longer holds any water. The rituals of life blind our eyes and monotonous chants cloud our consciousness. Are we a reflection of moments passed, or a reflection of time passed? An open soul holds no boundaries, holds no reality, and holds no obligation to time present or time past. The divine voice of God whispers to our soul. Will we open our hearts to spiritual love? We have become the water in our thirst for existence.

Will we breathe in the breath of creation and become one with spirit divine? In eternity of time, the voice of humanity will come and go. The great suffering of being human is the fear of being mortal. Oh, Kabir, will we ever break the cast of human norms and erase all lines of distinction? The beggar in us seeks the oneness of God. The priest seeks the oneness of God. The oneness of humanity seeks the oneness of God. Oh, Kabir, why do we not

seek the One who is oneness with
life and death? We are born
with a breath of God's wisdom,
the oneness of all reality.

Blind rituals lead to blind truth
and give humanity no wisdom in
redemption. A mind tangled in deep
thoughts will not hear the words of
God's wisdom. Oh, Kabir, what is
mankind, but a mirror of reality
which reflects no light? What they
look for and who they look for is
gazing at them with wide-opened
eyes. Will the spirit ever find
happiness in worldly needs? The
river of life is ever-changing with
time and flows silently in our
conscious stream. Kabir says, "The
darkness of night has opened
into day, but we have
not yet awoken from
our dreams."

Open Mind

The light of imagination lurks in the darkness of our minds and gives us the wisdom of truth in knowledge. The spirit of living is a world which we hold close to our hearts. In search of knowledge, passion is what moves us to seek and find. The beauty of our words is the nourishment for our soul. We have surrendered our will to time and life will walk through the world without hindrance. Our mind is like a forest: deep, dense, and mystical in reflection to itself. A beautiful mind is thoughtful, visionary, and moved by the vision of nature's beauty. We are known by our human faces but wear the mask of humanity to hide in our true Self.

The wind whispers in our ears to open our mind and see the elegance of nature's design. Stars give our mind to the universe of wonder, everlasting, ever inspiring. An open mind moves beyond its end and its beginning. In the deep stillness of reflection, all things move around the mind. A mind's ever-expanding vision pulls together the fragments of our whole. What holds us in our existence is the conscious awareness of our existence.

What brings us to realization is to
immerse ourselves in the holy water
of our being. The human mind
moves into the spirit to reveal the
deep emotions of our hearts. It is the
essence of light which wisdom
brings into our vision. A mind will
color our perception through the
senses and gives birth to our creative
imagination. A shallow mind
will drown our spirit and will no
longer hold the depth of meaning.
Will we ponder into our
mysterious nature and
unveil our mind
from duality of
dreaming?

Conscious Dream

Humanity is born in the moment and lives and dies for the moment. Time casts the infinite net to reality. We are like fish in water, trapped in our watery existence of life. Rivers walk into the ocean, like wandering souls walking into themselves. Love is the sweet fruit of life that binds man to woman. Will we breathe in the fragrance of nature? The hands of the wind are mystical and tender to flowers of the world. Humanity sleeps under the watchful eye of the night until the glorious sun awakens it to consciousness.

A blackbird sings the coming of dawn's light and calls us to come out of our dreamy existence. The morning dew clings to every blade of grass, glistening and translucent in the light. Under the vastness of the conscious world, nature becomes the spark of human awareness. The sun rises over purple-hazed clouds, lifting the veil of darkness, revealing the splendor of creation. The miracle of life is God's gift to humanity, a conscious dream for human salvation.

Let There Be Wisdom in Truth

Of Substance

The world is born in our
consciousness to fulfill
our human role. The beauty
of reality settles in our imagination,
but the truth of perception betrays
our soul. True wisdom only
grows with time if we
remain humble in our
existence. The words of
our mind remain empty
until they are filled
with truth of
substance.

On Fire

The power of imagination
sets the world on fire. The
brush of inspiration paints
reality which vision longs
to acquire. If we have no
purpose in life, then does
it matter if we live or die?
A mind that is illuminated
with power of wisdom
glows with life in
a candle's eye.

Deep Ocean

In the deep ocean lies
the sediments of human
needs. On tall steep mountains
the footsteps of humanity
climb with slow cautious
speed. Swallowed whole
in one vision of conscious
awareness, the spirit sees
the wholeness of reality.
What is perception but
a broken dream, a
broken fragment of
our mortality?

Oppressed Freedom

Consciousness escapes through human virtue and gets caught in the web of worldly power. Freedom oppressed by the willful hands of humanity wall themselves into their narrow existence. We become prisoners in time the moment we are born. The face of evil is the ugly truth of our being which we no longer see. The pain in suffering is the pain which humanity no longer feels. The joy in happiness is the air which we choose not to breathe. The wisdom in simplicity is lost when we choose to live in the complexity of our needs. The knowledge which we seek makes us less wise the moment our pride clouds our intelligence. The more worldly life becomes the less time we have living in our moments.

The more we chase unfulfilled dreams the less time we spend on things that we cherish and hold. Human emotions lay wasted on never-ending pleasures, and the suffering of spirit is the fate of our own doing. We can no longer become human once the wisdom of our purpose is lost. Like a fallen leaf, we turn inward and outward only to back to the roots of our beginning. The power of the human spirit is silence which holds us sacred. The strength of human character is the collective realization

of our fragile existence. The
salvation for life is to overcome
the pain in our worldly suffering.

The deep well of humanity no longer
holds the water for our thirst. Time
is the beacon of our mortality if we
live life in our righteous ways. Life's
journey is the steps we take toward
the road to our end. True faith will
wash away our worldly dust. It is the
truth in wisdom which will help us
see the beauty of our spiritual being.
Why do we hold precious wealth
and fame which will come and go?
What is there left to hold when
giving up the world is what
makes us want it more? Time
is the withering spirit of our
existence, the rust of experience
so clings to our age.

The hands of creation mold our
humanity, but the will to be free is
our natural state. The vision of self
reflects in our eyes, but it is love
which deepens the mystical world.
The human will moves the footsteps
of humanity and paves the road
to reach all corners of time. A
wandering spirit cannot be
oppressed and seeks freedom
to walk into the world unbound.
The conscious eye will
awaken us from our
dreams and everything
we look for will
surely be found.

Let There Be Wisdom in Truth

A Desert Night

The wind wanders through the desert; carved in dunes are the waves of unforgiving reality. The hot blistering sun is soaked in every grain of sand, a lifeless canvas of the desert landscape. The vast open sky, cloudless, and infinite blue creates an oasis of reflected illusions. The morning mist rises and dwindles with time. The great body of the desert moves like waves in yellow-gold twisting rivers. The fast-moving wind blows into the dunes, like a great bamboo flute, emanating with a subtle melody of mystical sound. The desert lives, grows, and changes before our eyes.

We get lost and forget our existence in this sea of sand. The soul of nature is swallowed into far-reaching desert storms. The footsteps of life are the caravan of our journey traced in lines of sand. Harsh and bewildering, the desert becomes our all-encompassing and all-consuming world. The desert twilight sparkles in the mist of light, like diamonds which reflect the mystical glow into the heart of darkness.

The soul of night rests in our eyes and the deep universe becomes entrenched in desert dreams. The wind is weary as the night grows cold and tear-filled dewdrops bring life into desert flowers. The haunting

sound echoes in the distant and voices
the mystery of nature into our
sleeping souls. Will we listen to the
mystical voice of divine wisdom?
The symphony of music spreads
deep into the desert valleys. The
human spirit is mesmerized and
dazzled in the splendor of sound. It
is the beauty of nature for which we
yearn. A speck of light as distant
as any star penetrates darkness and
comes to rest eternally into our
poetic vision. In every grain of
sand, time measures our existence
and in every moment of reflection,
the desert holds us ageless.

We humble our humanity, close our
eyes, and immerse ourselves in the
serenity of nature's love. Lost are the
paths to our journey as the wind
erases the deep boundaries of our
human nature. We have become
phantoms in our illusions as we seek
the oasis of comfort in our desert
home. A thirst for water burns in our
mind as the heart seeks refuge from
the unforgiving eye of the desert sun.
It is the soul of the desert that we
must walk through to liberate our
human spirit. A voice of destiny is
calling our name, but we have
become lost in the desert
of dreams and no
longer can hear it.

All-consuming

God's nature is in every
fragment of the universal whole.
We hold our faith in our heart,
conscious wisdom for the blind soul.
Will we ever open our eyes
to the sacred moments of living?
Humanity can never grow until it
overcomes its humble beginning.
Are we not conscious, a mosaic
of infinite perception? The
beauty of the human spirit
is God's all-consuming
obsession.

Waste

The sweetness of fruit is never great
until the sweet tooth finds it too late.
How bitter become desires for
wealth when we waste life's
moments in time so great. Will we
keep seeking pleasures of the
world and become prisoners
in our seeking? What is the
true nature of happiness
which will stop the heart
from breaking?

Journey

If we forget our beginning, then we will find no beginning in our end. Our humble past is the enemy of tomorrow, but it is our present we must befriend. Will we ever give up our stubborn pride and walk toward our destined path? If we burn our humanity, then the spirit suffers in the fire of human wrath. The journey toward life is under the sole of our feet until we come back home to rest. Will we uproot our conscious mind and honor time as our sacred guest?

Well of Greed

The well of greed holds too much water for our thirst. Lured into it with ever-growing desires we fall into it headfirst. Humans will seek the world looking for unfound, hidden treasures. The fruit of happiness will not satisfy our simple pleasures. Is laughter in our soul enough to kindle the human spirit? The thirst for self-realization is infinite and gives our moments in time no merit.

Humanity

The footsteps of humanity have
walked the earth with eyes fully
opened. Human existence has moved
through time, but their will to
civility remains forever broken.
Humans have journeyed far
in all corners of this world.
In their history of wars, pillage,
and destruction to forsake
God with a bloody sword
they hurl. The will to empower
is the yearning of
humanity, which decays
with time our consciousness
morality. Oh, Nature!
Why do you keep giving
the world the beauty of
your soul and keep
forgiving the perils
of humanity?

The Way Into Tao

A mind anchored in Tao will pass through the web of reality without being caught. Like a river lost to the world, Tao will take her to the sea. Heaven and earth will reflect in each other, and Tao will holds them with light of wisdom. It is the yin-yang of reality that binds our fragments to the oneness of existence. Tao is the two extremes of one reality. Fish live in water and water lives inside the fish. Man breathes in Tao and is reborn with every breath. He who lives in caves of darkness sees only shadows in form. He who lives in Tao sees truth under the veil of darkness.

If we seek knowledge, then we will burden the mind with heavy thoughts. Tao seeks nothing and nothing seeks Tao. If we try to hold Tao, then we will go home empty-handed. If we try to hold our breath, then we will become empty of life. Tao is the way into us and a way out of us. The beads of external and internal reality are strings knotted in Tao. Light and darkness become one with Tao. Man and woman hold no form in Tao. If we run away from the truth, then Tao will find us in our house of lies. Power is the root of all human weakness and weakness is the power of evil. If we walk on the surface of our mind, then we will not sink into the depth of our learning. A reality that holds no vision needs no eyes. How do we feel without touch and touch without feeling? A mind without consciousness is lost to the senses.

The soul walks into the spirit, and the spirit walks into the soul; Tao walks in with no steps, with no burden under its feet. A man who hoards wealth welcomes thieves into his home. Kings who live in vanity die of moral decay. The rich who rob the poor have many locks on their doors. Tao grows rich in poverty, finds happiness in sorrow, and lives with no walls and doors. A tree that flaunts its beauty gets cut down; a river full of passion will overflow its banks. A flower that bleeds with colors will die in youth; a moth in love with light dies with eternal bliss. Tao will walk into the world and hold space in time and time in space. The footsteps of humanity walk into Tao and journey through life; Tao will guide them with grace.

Happiness

The will to happiness is to go beyond the walls of comfort. To be free is like an ever-changing river that moves with time. The pendulum of human emotions swings from love into despair and joy into sorrow. Human nature is bound to happiness and happiness is bound to human nature. The stream of conscious existence reflects on the surface of our needs. Happiness will move us in and out of reality. All great happiness comes through the doors of sorrow. The birth of our humanity will grow toward the light of contentment. What is happiness? Where is happiness? Does happiness truly exist? Will happiness linger long enough to be realized in our conscious awakening? The wings of freedom lift into the wind and echo in laughter that holds their glory.

Happiness will rise like the morning mist and unveil the beauty of being alive. We are the dewdrops of nature that cling to the surface of our colorful existence. A butterfly drifts in our imagination: light, serene, joyous, and becomes the spirit of nature. We hold our hands open and wide in the moment as happiness falls like raindrops on the tender soul. We have become the water in our thirst that we long to drink. A drop of eternity is all that we seek. There is no deep sea greater than our

world of joy. Happiness walks on
shallow ground but it is the depth of
our emotions that holds our reality.

The journey through time will take
us deep into our souls, leaving the
world in dust for the wind to collect.
Will we hear the echo of laughter
that brings happiness into our heart?
The serenity of silent moments will
whisper the true voice of happiness.
The humor of our mystical emotions
stirs laughter and breaks open the
walls to our soul. The mosaic of
our existence is reflected in
mirrors of our perception which
binds the fragments of time.
The face of humanity looks
silently toward the sky and
the sky reflects their fate at a
riverbed. Joy moves into
sorrow and sorrow moves
into joy and the
soul of happiness
the body weds.

Slow Down

If we run too fast in the world then
everything seems a blur in haste.
Slow down, hold your thoughts, and
give life your total affection and not
let it go to waste. Why chase the
tail of existence when the light of
wisdom holds no form? Sit still in

your thoughts, and keep the fire
burning in your heart to keep the
spirit warm. A ravenous but
thoughtful spirit will seek light
and keep wisdom from going
blind. True knowledge
is our immortal truth,
and the more we seek,
the greater is
our find.

Etched Moments

If we live in moments of our dreams,
then we will not look for reality
into tomorrow. Like rays of
happiness which breaks through
damp clouds, we will wash away the
storms of our sorrow. Silence will be
the unspoken words of wisdom as
we speak with our inner voice. A
warm summer breeze spreads the
love of nature and makes the heart
rejoice. Will we walk into
our moments with quiet
footsteps? The road
into life is etched in
time as memories
are pressed behind
in faded
steps.

Let There Be Wisdom in Truth

Wall of Ignorance

The soul is never at peace when the human spirit is filled with anger. A child grows with age, but it is our humble existence which keeps us younger. How do we break the wall of ignorance which we have built with our own hands? The mind is lost in thoughts and looks for wisdom in humanity which it can't understand. The human soul is trapped in our body, but the will to be free breaks through our imagination. Curiosity is the spark which will burn through our intellectual stagnation.

Morally Strong

A mind which wanders in idle thoughts moves back and forth in all directions. A life without purpose fears the real world and conforms willingly to all objections. If we remain still in our thoughts, then our spirit will have time to think with conscious awareness. The fragments of our existence come with time, but we must hold them in our mind to give us wholeness. The road to success will take us far from ourselves and the journey

will become narrow and long.
Those who are not afraid
to walk into the world gain
courage and in wisdom
grows morally
strong.

Enemy of Youth

Honesty is the light in a child's
wisdom but ceases to grow in man's
truth. Purity of the heart is stained by
the world and becomes the enemy of
youth. Aged with time are the human
rituals on ways of living. We have
become infinite in our needs, but
time holds limits and is unforgiving.
Do we look into the mirror of
self-reflection and only see
our opaqueness? A shadow
of reality can hide our form,
but light will reveal
our nakedness.

Faith Gives

Faith will heal the human spirit once we see into wisdom of divine creation. Brought into consciousness is the sweetness of nature's love. Faith in truth is in the virtue of life that lightens our footsteps toward our journey's end. Faith will touch our soul and become one with God's nature. Take in the breath of eternity and we will breathe out the dust of our existence. Thirst for living is the lifeblood of our spiritual salvation. Will we walk toward the river and see our reflection wandering into our eyes?

The oneness of faith moves the stream of consciousness towards the oneness of being. The limits of life look to the infinite and the infinite grow through God's expansive will. The vision of light is what keeps the night burning with love of mystery.

In the mold of human existence, the birth of God has taken many forms. Having faith gives us power over suffering and faith overcomes suffering when God is nearest to our soul. The mirror image of the two ends is like Enkidu in Gilgamesh through the love of Shamhat gives meaning to faith in friendship and sorrow. Faith gives hope and wisdom to our spirit and binds us closer to ourselves. Without faith, we are drifting dust in the wind, with no substance and no direction. Faith

gives our mind simple truth that
transcends reason and reality. Faith
takes away the darkness from our
world and gives light to our spiritual
being. How do we come to terms
with our humanity, but through faith
in wisdom that it conceived.
True faith goes beyond
rituals, beyond self and
remains spiritually
pure in a heart
which believes.

Let There Be Wisdom in Truth

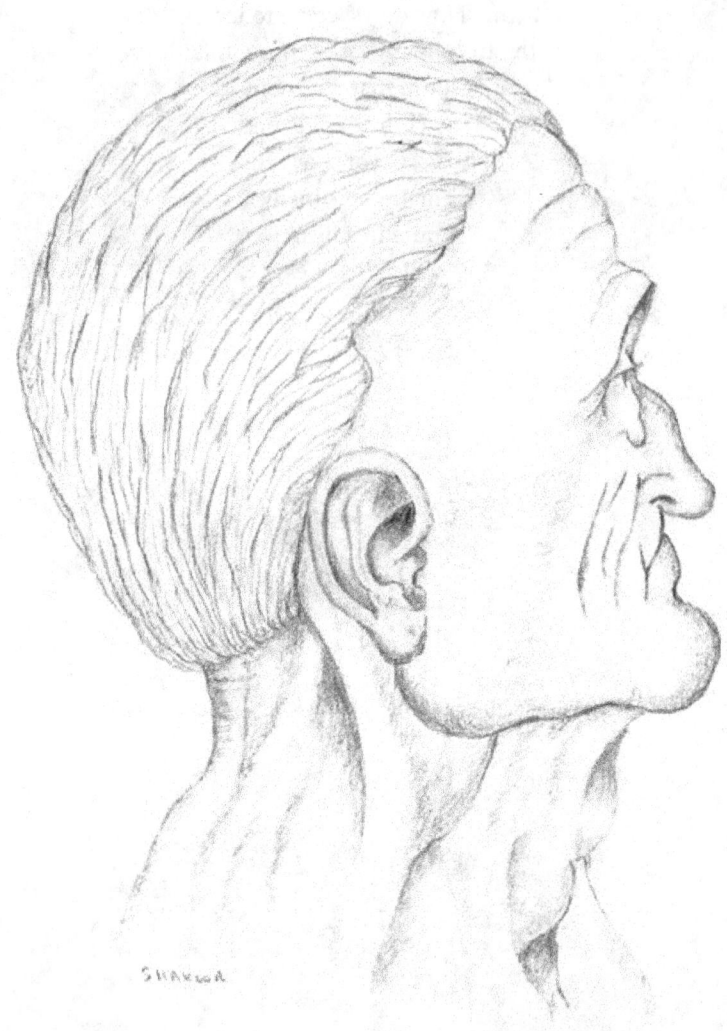

Vigor of Youth

Passing youth is Spring's blossom that time gives us to live in our journey through life. The vision of time is the vision of our inspired existence. Memories etched in moments reflect our past and casts shadows on our aged faces. Human emotions dipped in youthful laughter flow into the beauty of nature and move into our hearts. Will we walk into ourselves and open the doors to our souls? The passion of being human saturates our senses in the realism of life's simple truth. The face of nature looks at us with its silent gaze. The eyes of humanity will not open to nature's beauty until we bring love into our spirit.

We hold the world in our thoughts and our mind glows in the burning of imagination. A rose is the first miracle of nature's mystical and creative form. The wind is the gentle emotion which touches our senses and holds the joy of living with its first touch. Will we cleanse our soul in pearl-like raindrops of spring's first rains? The seeds of our beginning are growing toward their end, as youth ages with time. A poetic vision is spoken in words and gives meaning to our wide-mind perception of nature's unwritten reality. Eternity in every moment is our eternity of conscious awareness. We are forever bound to life as the

Let There Be Wisdom in Truth

spirit remains still in ever-moving times. The world is our song and dance and becomes the inner voice that calls to our center of being. Have we become a dream in our reality or a reality full of dreams? The glory of the sun warms our spirit. The deep blue sky reflects our emotions. The mood of the night glows into the moonlight with mysterious delight.

The universe becomes the wonder of our imagined will. The sea of distant stars we gaze in silent admiration. Oh nature, will you give us your vision of wisdom and humble us in our youth? It is your light that gives a face to humanity. It is the mirror of reality you hold which reflects the truth of our being. Have we not become prisoners in our worldly freedom? The bridge of time is the road between life and death. Are we the youthful spirit that hides in an old man's coat? Will we know the inner child that comes to the surface with ripened age?

There are moments in nature, when the red virgin rose lies frozen in the cold rocky world. The mind sees only what it wants to see. The body seeks pleasure when the soul suffers from moral sickness. Human nature fragments with entropy of life and the spirit gather the pieces to keep us whole. Thirst becomes our spiritual

need and water will comfort our
body of thirst. Life is the sculpture
of our youthful form as the hands
of our will erases them with age. In
wonder the imagination runs
wild with curiosity and worldly
knowledge will bring them to age.
Youth is the sensual fragrance of
humanity and true love will bring
them to age. Youth runs in our blood
with raw emotions, but the heart
will bleed them with age.

In the vastness of time lies the
vastness of our humanity. It is
the infinite of our moments
which remain infinite with our
sentiments. The vigor of love will
forever keep us deeply spirited.
We are born through love
and through love, we grow
forevermore. Oh youth, you ran
right through us and left us only the
aftertaste of your honey-sweet
moments. Were you a reality
of our dreams or a dream
that became our reality? Our
eyes open into consciousness
and awaken into the human
spirit. Oh youth, you fade
too quickly and all that is
precious no longer
holds any merit.

How Deep

The vastness of life seems full
and yet we still hold our spirit
in emptiness. The wealth of
the world is an empty bowl
when needs of the heart are
not filled with happiness.
We live in light of wisdom,
but it is the eyes of the
world which are blinded by
darkness. How deep is
our thirst for life and how
restless we have become in
moments of stillness? The
pleasures of life please us
not and yet we keep seeking
that which we can't find.
Why do we chase dreams
day and night only
to wake up blind?

All Will Go

Drift, oh wandering leaf, drift, and
fall to the earth with your silent
surrender. Were you not born
yesterday in the vigor of youth, a
fleeting moment in all your
splendor? The wind whispers
in a voice of mocking laughter the
power of human mortality.
All will be and all will not be one day;
there is no room to bargain for
immortality. We are anchored to

our consciousness; the soul is hidden
under the flesh of existence. Human
nature is the sweet fruit of spiritual
living, but it is God's creative
vision which gives life
its true substance.

Prisoners

Man will build walls to hold
freedom in his will to be
free. A caged existence has no
boundaries; the more we walk
into it, the less we will see. Will we
walk the road which is paved with
the hardships of life? The truth of
wisdom is gained when we liberate
our bodies from sorrows and strife.
Tear down the house which hides the
soul of freedom. What good is
power to the wealthy when
they become prisoners in
their own kingdom?

Life Dance

A dragonfly lands on a blade
of grass. Translucent wings cut
into the wind like hardened
brass. Silent and motionless
it looks down at its reflection
on the quiet surface of the water.

Let There Be Wisdom in Truth

The beauty of nature at its most
charming lures and betrays her.
Under the stillness of the pond,
a frog eyes the dragonfly
and waits for its chance.
A hawk flies above the surface,
dives through the sky and
catches the frog in its
flying dance.

Let There Be Wisdom in Truth

Light of Humanity

Human nature gives truth to reality and burns with passion in the heart of darkness. Humanity is the light in a candle's eye and glows warm, embracing the spirit of our existence. In our burning mind, the embers of emotions will fan the flame. We only live through sorrow that holds us to the touch. We live and die a thousand times to forge our destiny by wandering away from our beginning. We are born-again in the slumbering seed that opens with the coming of spring's rains. The music of life's mystical song will echo into the wind. The soul sleeps in the tranquility of unseen reality. The night will unveil and veil our darkness. Stars burn eternal in the vastness of space and keep night-time vigil. The light of creation will reveal the deep nature of our humanity.

Wisdom only comes when we open our eyes and see through the body of our human form. Why do we lose ourselves in a world that no longer exists? In the act of seeking we will be found and finding what we seek is no longer worth seeking. A river which meets the ocean is no longer a river but the ocean. Absorbed in the purity of divine love we come to our conscious surface and become the light of humanity. We seek love in our wandering hearts; we only find freedom in our open landscape. We wander with bliss under the vast blue sky and spread our arms in the glory of being born. We long to lose our spirit in a star-filled desert twilight. Where is the great love that we seek?

Will we open the doors into ourselves and let the light of spirit in? Is it not love which seeks us, but the soul which seeks love? Love takes root in spiritual wisdom and grows out into the world with simple glory. Beauty will calm the savage nature of our senses, but it is love that will make us human. Why do we drink the poison of hate and give evil room in our hearts? Will we ever lift the cloud of darkness from our eyes? Why do we keep running into the walls of reality which hold no freedom? The footsteps of our journey trace us back to our beginning, but it is time which lures us to our end. The path to mystical awakening takes us deep into life. We live in every moment and come home to rest from a world that has aged our weary soul.

The human story is written on pages of time, etched in wisdom of truth and hard-pressed in the consciousness of our mind. If we walk too far into reality, then all we will find is our shallow grave. Life is many colors of self-realization, many shades of meaning which come to vision with conscious perception. The fate of life is in the hands of our will. How do we hold the comforts of the world that are more elusive than the wind? Caught in the web of life, humanity can no longer bargain with death. Will we breathe in the splendor of the world and breathe out the excess of our existence? Will we move into ourselves to touch the reflection of truth that glows in our hearts? Time has become the broken wings of our destiny. The fragments of perception give wholeness to conscious life. Does the mind think that it can walk away from the truth without realizing it first?

It is the warm blood of humanity that is spilled by mankind. Human folly will burn the forest, and trees will embrace the flames with their forgiving nature. The dust of reality falls on our hands, as the wind scatters them into our imagination. Will we bring life into form and give our spirit the vision of creation?

Words of Silence

Silence escapes through our words and shatters the fragile reality of our existence. Do we have the moral courage to fight against the will of humanity? Words will hold our sentiments, and the mind will grow in our words. Pressed under the weight of tyranny, human virtues long to be free. Words which hold meaning lift the conscious spirit. Words which speak volumes are pressed in the pages of time. Will we walk between the lines of duality and give our steps the freedom to move? Time holds the wisdom of our beginning to free us from our end. We grow into our words when we take in our conscious world. A thirsty spirit needs no water. If we hunger for knowledge, then we will never go hungry. If we seek the truth, then the truth will find us in all that we seek.

Human eyes which look for mortality become the vision of their humanity. Will we listen to the voice of nature which sings the words of our heart? The poetry of our words is the beauty of nature. True wisdom is the knowledge we hold in our vision as we journey through life. A mind holds time still as thoughts race through our meaningful existence. Oh Humanity, what will become

of our spirit when we sell
our souls for the world? Will
we see the illusions of reality with
our perception and erase the lines
between sanity and insanity?

If we walk silently and seek our
life's purpose, then we will grow
into ourselves. Will the body reflect
on the mirror surface of our soul?
What will be written on the empty
pages of time are the hard lessons of
life. Who are we and what is it that
makes us human? God's truth is the
love of humanity and true faith is the
love of God. Will we walk toward
light and open the doors to our
hearts? It is our humanity which
marches into the destined path of
life. It is the heavy emotions which
drown our words. It is the sound of
birds which awoke us to see the
majesty of dawn's light. It is silent
moments in time which pull us to the
center of our being. The conscious
eye opens the mind into reality,
but our human nature is still
blind to wisdom in
what it is seeing.

Gluttony

We have become blind to our world
and virtue is nowhere to be found.
The conscious soul holds its tongue

and words come to the surface with
no meaning, no sound. Lost in our
spirit is the courage which wisdom
gave to transcend darkness. Will we
ever find the cure which ails our
moral sickness? We come to destroy
the sacred testaments of God's
prudence with no guilt and
no reflection in morality.
What is civilization, but
gluttony of infinite
greed, the eternal
abyss toward
insanity?

A Guest

A guest comes to your door, a
gift from God, welcome him
with open arms. On the first day,
a guest of joy, the second day oh
boy, and the third day loses all its
charm. True compassion warms the
heart and the spirit will grow with
empathy. What is it which makes
us human is kindness and sympathy.
The light which illuminates the soul
is the guest we welcome with our
heart. Give them more than what
you would give yourself,
pure kindness
from the start.

Human Grace

Human grace is born through a life of sorrow and gives us the vision of happiness toward tomorrow. Wisdom is gained with humility when we give back what we borrow. If we give ourselves to others, then we will receive so much more. Life is a gift like no other that keeps us strong in our spiritual core. True purpose in life is given to a soul that is not afraid of hardship. We are liberated from our suffering when we give ourselves to the faith we worship.

Evil Uprooted

The moral shame of humanity cannot escape the conscious soul and finds no place to hide from guilt. The backbone of moral courage is in our deed of righteous conduct upon which a strong character is built. The wisdom of what we believe will guide us toward the moral path to self fulfillment. The spirit of living will give us peace once we remain true in our ethical commitments. If we remain silent and allow evil to spread then it will come back

Let There Be Wisdom in Truth

to infect us in venomous ways.
The collective consciousness
of human morality will uproot
evil to give it no voice
and time of day.

Let There Be Wisdom in Truth

Burning Love

Oh, fair-minded beauty you have stolen our hearts with your mystical smile. In the silent darkness of night, your vision burns like stars with their everlasting glow. You bring your vision of beauty and awaken the spirit of our eyes. Like waves in the ocean, your sensuous emotions flood the soul with overflowing passions. It is the curls in your hair that capture subtle shades of light and gives your face their pearly glow.

Tender desires grow in the soft moonlit night as nature carves your form into an artistic dream. The fragrance of your body flows through the majestic wind and awakens the senses to love of being. In God's divine vision your spirit was brought into the light to give the world its poetic reality. Like dew in the mist that clings to the lips of earthly flowers, you cling to our soul with an everlasting need to love. Dawn breaks the will of night as the glorious sun moves above the horizon and finds you sleeping like a delicate rose.

To love you a thousand times is to live for you in each and every moment of eternity. A heart is all emotions, the mind is full of serenity, and the spirit burns under the warmth of your touch. We have

become prisoners in your eyes and
the pain from a bleeding heart can't
overcome the joy. It is the vision of
your face that burns with passion.
Desire fan the flames, and embers
glow in our smoldering soul.

Love burns in our eyes a thousand
nights until her beauty comes into
the vision of our dreams. Dear Lord,
what was it that made you fall in
love with humanity? Did you not
sacrifice your great soul to liberate
man from their suffering? A candle's
light is divine as it glows and
flickers in her soft black pearly eyes.
If you are lost to us, then blind
existence is our abyss. Dear love!
Will you make us walk the world
like a wandering mystic, holding the
empty bowl in our quivering hands?
Unfulfilled love becomes mystical
and once fulfilled becomes human.
Oh Lord, were you not the
bridge to love that binds
man to woman?

Heavy Steps

It is through hardship that happiness will find its true worth in joy. The whole of existence is in life of simplicity that power will come to destroy. Infinite needs will bury our spirit and drown the beauty of life's essence. Why walk with heavy steps and take the mind far into the world and cover no distance? Time will bargain with no one and in its vastness, our fate will be the same. We will come to dig our graves when we give ourselves to wealth, power, and fame.

Guest for a Day

Life-consuming desires for pleasure will bring great suffering when we go blind. The well of need is infinite, the deeper you go the less you will find. A bowl of water is all that we need, but we thirst for the ocean that we can't drink. Wisdom holds our words in silence as the mind speaks, but can't think. Countless faces have

come and gone; no one is
here to stay. We are born
to live and live to die;
humanity is but a
passing moment,
a welcomed guest
for a day.

Hasty Steps

If we are hasty in our steps,
then we will stumble and fall
to the ground. Breathe in wisdom,
slow and deep, toward the spirit
we are bound. Will we take
time to reflect and open our
minds to the truth no longer
found? If we listen to the voice
of nature, then consciousness will
awaken the soul with its mystical
sound. We will grow old before
our time if we let our spirit
become too worldly. In
our fast-moving world,
time will take flight
and quickly pass over
our life's journey.

Shadow in Form

Darkness will rob us of
light and wash away the
shadow of our form. The
laughter of the world will

mock humanity and silence
our emotions; a burst of
passion for our inner
storm. Morality will
move consciousness into
our moral ways. The
journey through time will
uncover the truth of human
praise. The words of the heart
are like rivers; they flow down
toward the greater whole.
Time will escape through
our hands and fall into
life's empty bowl.

Seeking

Will we ask the question which
has no answer and remain
intellectually versed? The clay
bowl is half-filled with wisdom
and half-empty with our thirst.
The fragments of our dreams
settle like illusions into our
consciousness. Life becomes
layered in time, but the great
love of giving must remain
anonymous. Will we walk
on our destined path and carry
the purpose of existence
which we inherit? What
are we seeking which takes
us deep into the darkness
of our human
spirit?

Delusions of Power

Power looks to immortality and blinds the mortal soul in seeking what time will come to destroy. It is the irrational which becomes rational with power. The needs of humanity leaves the spirit wanting more the pleasures of this world. What we can hold is hope to free ourselves from the bondage of desires. It is the will of power which takes away our conscious morality. There is great wisdom in poverty which humbles the spirit and makes it strong. A simple soul lays power to its feet and walks all over it. Why do we hold ourselves captive in want of power?

Trapped in the noose of reality, escape is to let go of ourselves from the lure of worldly pleasures. It is the mind which reflects through stillness, holding nothing but quiet thoughts. Power is seductive and will bleed men of their morality. It is the hand of greed which pulls us in; the more we want the less we will have. Power becomes most controlling when we

become weak in our moral
conscience. The delusions
of holding power distill the
mind, magnify the perception
of self and robs the spirit
of peaceful existence.

Breath of Air

The world is infinite beauty of colors which stir our emotions like a gentle breeze which touches nature's heart. We live in our conscious world as we grow into the spirit of being human. How do we live for the moral truth in wisdom which takes our breath away? If we spread the wings of freedom beneath our will then the spirit will soar into the sky with all its glory. Take in the breath of air and the wisdom of breathing will calm our senses. Will we look inside with soulful eyes and see the beauty of our mystical spirit?

Endless are life's needs which trap us in unending pleasures of the world. Will we walk in our conscious steps to move toward our destined path? Will we hold our mind with light thoughts and give our words their eloquent voice? If we anchor the self to the body, then the spirit of being can never be free. Conscious will is an impression of our consciousness and cannot overcome the desires of human nature. Life's blood runs in our veins toward our heart but too quickly bleeds when reality cuts very deep into our mind, body, and spirit.

How do we overcome emotions which drown us in our deepest moments of yearning? Where do we go to find calmness in our wildest storms? The grace of our existence is the light of wisdom. To live outside of ourselves, we must look inward for self-realization. The steps in our journey are etched in time, impressed in memories which reflect our passing existence. Can we hold the world in our hearts and never let it go? Will we hold ourselves in a world that no longer holds ground? The fragments of our existence become the edges of our consciousness which seeks to become whole. The seeds of reality become the roots of our being as we branch out in search of meaning and purpose. Have we become too stagnant in our spirit which can't step away from the nature of being human?

The soul of non-existence is what comes before and what comes after our existence. If we are the miracle of divine creation, then what is the substance of our creative soul? The breath of humanity is the consciousness of God's will. If we breathe in the wisdom of our essential truth, then we shall live in harmony with our worldly nature. How sincere is our love for truth is measured in the moral virtue of how we live. The light of the world will reflect in our spirit once we open our mind's eyes. A breath of air will cleanse the soul and consciousness

Let There Be Wisdom in Truth

will breathe consciousness
to grow humble
and wise.

Virtuous Truth

The soul of morality is our sacred truth, untouched, virginal, and necessary for growth of the human spirit. Why fight for the great truth in justice when laws have lost their virtuous merit? Heaven and Earth set the boundaries for our spiritual growth. Why do we hide behind the veil of truth, the naked reality under human clothes? Will we come out into the world and expose the two faces of human morality? The duality of human nature will hold good and evil in one hand, but with the other will bargain for the soul of our humanity.

Less Spoken

The human spirit is born to live and live it must only to die for the spirit of all things. Dear Lord, give us faith in reason to open the wisdom of truth which you bring. A heart's love is absolute and not afraid of being broken. Words which remain silent under our lips hold weight when they are less spoken. We are

guests in time infinite,
a speck of flickering dust
in our unsteady gaze. Will
we grow old under our
skin and come back
to our simple ways?

Emotional Reality

What fills life's empty cup is
the vision of pure perception.
The human spirit has lost its moral
virtue in wisdom and lives in
illusions of worldly deception.
We walk blindly on the surface
of our conscious journey, looking
for the road to salvation. Will
we continue to run in circles,
chasing the wind heavy with
near exhaustion? The will to
conscious being awakens the
mind and moves us into our
emotional reality. The will
to be human catches the
mind in its web of reason,
and to escape is vain
banality.

Silence Breaks

A cold night's mist settles on morning dew and the conscious world opens its eyes upon awakening. A crow breaks its silence at dawn's light and echoes the joyous coming of the well-timed morning. The trees stand unmoved as the sun's golden light seeps through slumbering leaves. The clouds burn in a red-orange-purple haze as the sun rises over the horizon and the beauty of nature sighs and heaves. Time holds still our dreams and eyes open to the world in conscious glory. Nature's beauty is boundless, graced with spiritual wisdom and divine allegory.

Let There Be Wisdom in Truth

Power Over Power

Power is malignant to the mind, becomes a disease to the soul, and destroys the basic values of humanity. When kings live in luxury, the poor are often made to suffer. The will of power sheds light on human nature. Those who yearn for supremacy weaken their power to reason. A nation which is built on power will break the camel's back. When a lion roars, the hyena breaks its silence with laughter. When elephants trample on ground the ants are nowhere to be found. A king's arms which hold too tight to power often suffocate the ones who are too close. Ignorance among the masses is the secret to holding power and all who remain blind are powerless to see beyond. Justice fragments with tyranny and human morality dies when power becomes the savage nature of humanity. Power breeds power, like dust which collects dust under our feet. The voice of civilization is the collective power of the masses. Power over power is to embolden the human spirit to let go of power which can only make you powerless.

Power leads to great suffering and with power, we become prisoners in our suffering. The human soul which anchors itself to power becomes cold-blooded and can never achieve greatness. The wisdom for salvation is to resist the temptation of power. Power is the illusion of immortality and mortality the delusion of our immortality. Can power ever give us the strength to escape death? When humanity chases power it only hastens its end. Power moves us toward God, and we strive for power to become God. Power is the blood of nobility and only nobility is ordained with the right to hold power. This is the great lie, the disease, and incest of noble blood. Power is divine and only the most powerful hold the divine wisdom to subjugate the weak. Power is the hand of destruction which builds and destroys great empires. If we believe in the purity of reason, then the power of the mind will break the walls of vanity. Human history is plagued by want of power and once gained can't sustain its humanity.

Fading Footsteps

The heart and soul become heavy in their journey when the mind strays too far into time. If we trace our moving steps through our reflective eyes, then we will carve the path toward our existence. The fate of life is realized with every breath we take. Take in the wisdom of reality and our breath will calm the senses. Why burden our hearts with emotions when the purity of love will lift the spirit? Dance like a lily and the joy of the world will rest beneath our feet. Time holds us in our moments of reflection as consciousness echoes the laughter of passing days.

The face of reality has no eyes and the vision of humanity has no face. A stagnant soul ages with time like an unyielding rock, stubborn and unbroken. What is the impulse that moves our feet? How far will we go from the center of our being? The surface of our existence is lined with change as we grow old and wise in the spirit of time. The sediments of awareness become the wisdom in our collective whole. Time scatters like dust in the wind and settles on the conscious moments of our being. A journey through life moves inward as the vision of an observing mind erases all boundaries of certainty. We can no longer walk on the shallowness of time; our lives have become too deep and heavy to the world. Will we open the door to our soul and walk toward the center of our being? In the vastness of eternity, we are humbled by our space in time. Etched in time are the fingerprints of humanity. We move with time, and restless becomes our spirit as the mind holds us still in the great depth of our perception. A path into our consciousness has no end and no beginning. A life which has no vision of existence finds no value in time. The human spirit that lives blind wanders in all directions but covers no ground.

We live and die a thousand deaths when we seek too much comfort in our wealth. A moment of time is our existence as we stroll through the world in search of our place and purpose. Will our penetrating eyes ever find true love in moments of endless searching? Who is the guest that stirs the emotions of our soul? We hold the world in our hands, but it is the will of time that can take it away. It is our mystical nature which moves the spirit to find grace in truth. A child is born in purity of spirit but grows old tainted by worldly existence. We come of age as we journey through time. Memories race through our inward eye and fragment our moments in time. We are born to live and live we must in

our spirit of living. The
human spirit will achieve
great wisdom if they
accept life's short
misgivings.

Blood of Humanity

Do we have the courage to defend
the dignity of our nation? Only a
coward hides behind the walls of his
station. Will we break our silence
when hypocrisy covers the truth
with blind lies? The voice of wisdom
soothes the tormented soul, which
lays broken and crying. The blood
of humanity runs in our veins and
spills into the world tainted and
flawed. Oh, civilization, the
will of our nation is the
divine and moral
character
of God.

Firm Ground

Those who take pride in knowing the
truth overwhelm their mind in the
vastness of what they are seeking.
Moral character will hold our feet
firm even when the ground beneath
our world is sinking. How can we

come to terms with humanity when
we are no longer human? Wisdom
will erase the boundaries of truth
between man and woman. The
will to know is our act of being
human from the start. Words
will gain their power once
they are spoken
from the heart.

Being True

The wealth of a nation is not in
the acquisition of power but in the
diversity of intellectual thought.
True power rests in words of
reason and justice which are
earned, never bought. The
spirit of freedom is born when
the collective consciousness of
humanity becomes a single voice.
Morality is the soul of civilization
which uplifts the human burden
and in happiness to rejoice. True
power holds no might; compassion
is the heart of a nation, and wisdom
is gained once pride is unfurled.
A nation which is true to
itself builds no walls,
opens its doors to
the needs of
the world.

Emotions in Knots

The footsteps of humanity walk on sacred ground and move toward their worldly end. Oh, Silent One, you speak so elegantly the truth of wisdom sent. Will we open our mind to the world which holds us in mystical thought? Nature has unveiled her colors and beauty twists and ties our emotions in knots. What is there to life, but a moment which binds us to reality? Oh, conscious man, were you not moved by the soft whisper which revealed your humanity?

No Vision! No Light!

The hidden well of knowledge takes us deep into ourselves where wisdom holds no light. What happens to our vision of reality when our consciousness can't see what's wrong and what's right? Will we live in our existence and hold our joy in life's rhythmic dance? The blood of humanity runs deep in our veins and gives life over death a fighting chance. Our thirst for knowledge is greater than the ocean, but it is the only water we can drink. The words of reality are no longer written on

Let There Be Wisdom in Truth

    our mortal existence, and
      the mind has lost
        its capacity
         to think.

Nature of Time

Will we walk with the steps of time, to become guests of this world? The moral road is steeply sloped like rugged mountains as we climb through our existence with staggering feet. The quest for immortality will leave us empty and unfulfilled. We will live and die in our humanity a thousand times before we become truly human. It is our beginning that holds us still, but it is our end that moves us further. Willed by time, the spirit is uprooted by reality and the perception of change becomes the water under our feet.

The great soul moves against our will, and the mind holds still the nature of time in motion. The gravity of our spirit laments the coming-of-age, but it is the burden of being human that rubs under the soles of our feet. Lingering in our consciousness are echoes of a thousand moments, and the lost vision of thousands of forgotten faces. Etched in fading time are memories that once were real. The story of our existence is written in our eyes as the vision of reality becomes endless time, endless searching. In silent moments of reflection the destiny of our journey reaches its final crossroad. What path we take in life will bind us to the oneness of our being.

Let There Be Wisdom in Truth

Memories crumble with time
in hands that hold them too long.
The inner searching is like flashes
of light, rapidly moving through
streams of consciousness and
settling like dust in our quiet mind.
The closer we move into our being,
the farther we walk away from the
world. The strength of our will
breaks through all limits of reality.
Will we open our eyes to bring
in the light that awakens our
consciousness? This ever-
bending universe folds and
unfolds under our feet. Can
we ever walk deep into
the forest of dreams
where the soul and
spirit can finally
meet?

Let There Be Wisdom in Truth

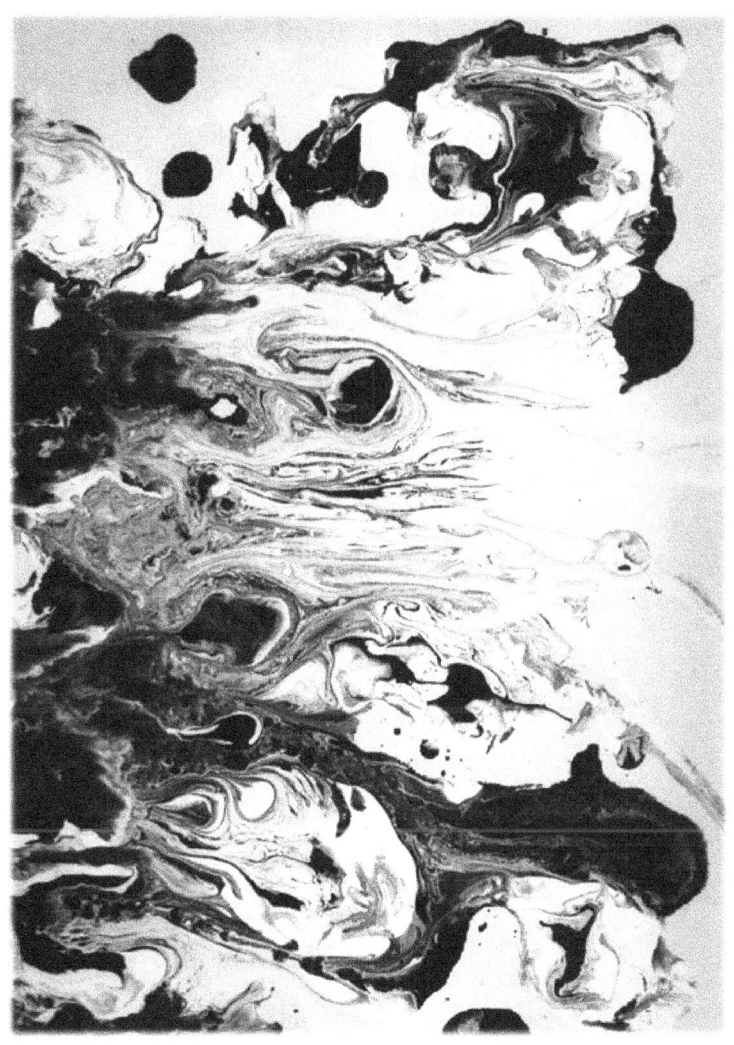

The Glass Reality

The naked face of humanity no longer reflects the light of wisdom. The eyes of reality look upon us with sadness and despair. The edge of time cuts deep into the human experience and lines our faces with too many emotions. The mask of humanity hides our consciousness and will not unveil our inner truth. We seek worldly pleasures to fill our spiritual emptiness. A mind plagued with distorted perception no longer brings human virtues to the surface. We become prisoners in our thinking and slaves to the power of our will.

The mirror of inner reflection brings to bear the pride on our face. The voice of reason silences our words and tries to come to terms with the after-effects of willful existence. How can we look into our face when there is too much darkness in our eyes? Humbled by the vastness of eternity, we look into the mirror with a browbeaten face. Can we see beyond our conscious mind and unmask the facade of our being? We learn the truth in wisdom by remembering the antiquity of our past. We learn the art of happiness by living through our world of sorrow. We learn humility when we give up vanity and become simple in our existence.

If we truly want to grow, then
we must unlearn what we have
learned. Worldly treasures will bring
poverty to the human spirit. The
deception of human nature is felt
by the heart and the guilt of
consciousness will not hide the truth.
We have aged before our time and
chasing empty dreams takes us fast
into our graves. We hold precious our
youthful form, but it is the hand of
time which takes it away. Is it the
want of freedom which traps us in
our will? We must overcome
ignorance to free the spirit from
being too human. How do we
clothe our naked reality with
human needs? How do we give
meaning to our non-existence?

Within our spirit is the nature of our
true self. Within infinity lies the
wisdom of finite existence. Why do
we carry the burden of living and
make our spirit too heavy to
support? Why look into a mirror
which looks back at us with cynical
eyes? What is left in the voice of
time is the silent murmurs of our
passing moments. What is left in
our words is the harmony of music
which moved our hearts. The sacred
journey of life will give our
imagination the glory of our dreams.
The dormant seed will one day bear
fruit to our ripened age. The inner
eye will awaken and take in the
wisdom of our world. Will we

shatter the glass reality with our
hardened spirit? The nakedness
of humanity morality will
not cover, and human
dignity will give
it no merit.

Invisible Web

Oh wounded pride, you salt the
wounds that burn with want of
vanity. All-consuming passions trap
us in our emotions and can never
free us from humanity. We run away
in fear of being caught in the
invisible web of reality. Will we ever
open our minds to the perception of
nature's duality? The power of will
moves us to walk on our destined
path, and we burn through time
with unconscious speed.
Man's bewildered soul
wanders, looking for
direction in life's
sacred creed.

Conscious Eye

Will we gather our awareness
and become conscious of our
shallow existence? A mind
runs too fast and the soul

can't hold wisdom still,
as the human spirit
surrenders without
resistance. Calm emotions
full of sentiments walk
silently into our heart
and quietly rest in our
dreams. The light has
opened the conscious
eye to sow reality
in our perception,
torn at the seams.

Eternal Truth

Truth is universal and holds no
boundaries and walks on solid
ground. It is like listening to music
which brings harmony and rhythm to
simple sound. We walk toward our
moral truth with the virtue to know
right from wrong. The consciousness
of humanity will overcome fear and
bring evil to light and remain
strong. The wisdom of truth shall
free the mind and life will
be judged by what is right.
The eternal truth
is timeless and will
beat in our heart
day and night.

One Night

The rich will spend their lives hoarding wealth which death will come to collect. Time so moves like an ageless river, a moment of life in one second to reflect. Infinite is the immensity of time which our dreams will see in one night. Will we ever wake up and come out of our dreams into the light? Why do we chase the wind which is bound in stillness? Will we walk away from the world and give up our pleasures to overcome worldly darkness?

Nature Divine

Oh, nature, sublime is your beauty which holds our heart in silent wonder. Humanity will do you no harm; it is your spirit which we seek to plunder. Infinite and varied are the colors that you bring into the human soul. Our thirst is never fulfilled as we keep pouring sweet nectar into our bowl. What is life, but a moment of passing, which nature gives us with love. Divine is heaven when mystical purity is breathed into nature from God above.

Conscious Journey

The spirit sleeps under the mystical glow of twilight and nature voices to the soul the secrets of eternity. We wash away moments of time as dreams take us deep into consciousness. Will we cleanse our emotions in the silence of the night and open our eyes to reflect on distant stars? Memories are the lost relics of reality which drift into our mind and settle on the surface of conscious time. The whole of earthly existence is dipped in gray silver moonlight and becomes our mystical dream, worth a thousand nights. The motion of our vision is like a river that flows quietly into the human soul. Will humanity ever open its eyes to the self they want to be? Will the spirit take root in reality and grow beyond its spiritual making? The conscious eye sees no boundaries between I and We.

Awake! Take flight into your everlasting glory. Will we take a moment to smell the fragrance of life before it's taken away by the moving wind? A rose which sleeps in our conscious dreams holds us sacred. The star's light is distant and eternal but will come to rest in our eyes. A forest listens to the sounds of living creatures and gives comfort to them with her elegance and grace. It is the will of the wind which moves clouds and stirs the slumbering trees. The

Let There Be Wisdom in Truth

darkness of the world is our deep abyss, and nothing moves until it is moved. The light of dawn spreads through the horizon and the mist of night rises into the sky. The beauty of light clings to our form and becomes the shadow of our dim existence. We are bound to nature and our true spirit is what binds us to wisdom. The colors of the world fall on the canvas of our dreams. The steps of our journey move through time and reflect the shallowness of our conscious stream.

Book of Pages

Books are bound to their pages and stand soundless, pressed in time. A curious mind opens them with loving hands to kindle their imagination. Books stacked on shelves stand like motionless trees holding the wisdom of humanity written in words. Will we open and look inside to give reverence to our intellectual curiosity? The sweet harvest of knowledge is pressed on every page, every word, and in every story. Will we know and learn the hidden meaning between the lines? The history of the human spirit is written on every page; the voice of the past is etched in every word.

Deep in thought, rich in spirit is the innovative mind which gave language its creative force. Human emotions written in a poet's mystical eyes unfold with every metaphor. Love for humanity is no easy task for Shakespeare. The wastelands of reality come through T.S. Eliot's mind. The romantic vision of love is Lord Byron's dilemma. Will we travel in adventure of human drama and fight the windmill of illusions which masks Don Quixote's follies? The world of redemption is Jean Valjean's hunger for bread.

Will you open me into your soul? I am all-knowing, all- saying, and my verses are written in words that speak of human wisdom. The envy of self once realized will lose its moral character. The want of being human is not the monster inside Frankenstein. The guilt of mind is the human need to become divine. Tangled in a web of conflict, only Dostoyevsky can help us escape our moral torments. An examined life is lived for truth in wisdom; Socrates was found guilty of being too wise. The nature of friendship is shared thoughts in letters to Lucilius. Being true to your nature is the only friend of humanity. Oh, Seneca, do we truly know how to be happy, to live and act with moral virtue? Is it a dream or an allegory which becomes the nightmarish reality of dreams? A nation that throws books in a fire, burns its moral character, and becomes ashes of civilization. The circle of life is our mystical dance, like the whirling words of Rumi's poetry. The soul of poetry is the fragrance of our existence

Will we wash our form in the purity of love with our everlasting soul? Oh, Kabir, did you not forget your rituals in search of unwritten faith? A river flows into the distance: the substance of real and unreal become one with our consciousness. The Overcoat is the comfort of humanity and becomes the destructive will of our envious nature. Curiosity will

Let There Be Wisdom in Truth

take us away from home to live
and learn the lessons of life. Oh,
Siddhartha, why overcome suffering
when suffering is the first step to
nirvana? Will we bleed into our
existence and cut through our
emotions to become whole with
ourselves? Oh, Dante, is humanity
the nightmarish reality of God's
creative will? It is human virtue
that sustains us with guilt before
we are born. It is the shadow in
Plato's cave, the truth which
gives form to light of reason.

Pressed in thoughtful words are the
books of human folly. Layered
between every page is the fate and
vision of reflection. An open book is
like a spirit which is free to wander
into the depth of human mind.
Humanity that is not fond of books
is like a heart that is not fond
of being loved. Oh, Erasmus, the
story of humanity is written in
every book, the humanistic
wisdom is what you
wrote and the
spirit approved.

Free Willed

The spirit will overcome the depth of sorrow once it gives itself to love of joy. Why waste life seeking perfection when simplicity will give us more to enjoy? Walk into our first step free-willed, for a journey through life takes a lifetime to complete. The rhythm of life rests in our hearts, and the music of the world is soulful and sweet. True happiness only exists for those who breathe in the gentle wind. If we look into the mirror and face the light, then the sound of laughter is all that we will find.

Love of Nature

Deep in the woods, we walk as time holds ground and nature extends the hand to our inner child. The face of humanity holds no ill grace as nature shapes the spirit which is unformed and wild. The forest is the body in the soul of nature, as the mystic beauty becomes the mist of reality under the uplifted sky. We are the seeds of creation rooted like trees to our creative imagination. Will humanity ever come out of its hidden surface and listen to nature's

poetic inspiration? Will we breathe
in the soul of nature and break the
silence of our hindered mind?
The truth of perception gives
birth to our reality and
what we love in nature
is all that we
will find.

Worldly Soul

An empty soul has its own
storms and weakens the spirit with
coming-of-age. Our mind is
anchored to time and moments of
conscious living become our worldly
stage. A child is born to become a
man, an unwelcomed guest. We
walk into the world to move toward
tomorrow, the footsteps of time are
hard-pressed. A humble life lived in
simplicity holds the spirit light and
carries no burden. A worldly
soul becomes a prisoner
with time and will not
move beyond the
lines of freedom.

Emotions of Love

Wings of serenity long for the sky;
fly from thy hand, my sacred dove.

Let There Be Wisdom in Truth

In truth, we are not bound by
abstracts of reason but consumed by
the emotions of love. Beauty which
we see brews and burns our form.
The moment we look into truth our
mind will no longer perceive it
beyond moral norms. Faith will be
our guiding light to wisdom and will
give love back to the spirit above.
Only through God's poetic
vision can humanity
becomes human
thereof.

Let There Be Wisdom in Truth

Nature of Love

Love is the sensuous breeze which warms the heart to the splendor of our world. In every movement of time, we are transformed, totally absorbed in the oneness of our nature. Beauty which beholds our eyes is the reflection of our soul. Live in the wonder of life and the human spirit becomes the sacred words of poetic reality. What mountains are we not able to overcome in pursuit of great love? Love bridges the gap between body and spirit. The purity of life distills into our hearts and gives love its eternal grace. Love is redemption for the sacred human soul.

A desire for pleasure diminishes the spiritual nature of love. Will we know the eternal mystery of love which spills over with mystic emotions? The ivory glow of a thousand stars will reflect in the darkness of our eyes. Love that touches the soul becomes infinite and complete in the wholeness of time. The craving thirst for life is our reason for living. Love clings to our spirit like morning dewdrops clinging to mother earth. It is nature's beauty which makes the heart beat faster. Sumptuous is the sweet white lily which makes the fragrance of love sacred to the wind. "Hold me in your eyes," the sweet lily cries under the light of day and

night. The graceful dove lifts from
our open hands and frees love from
human desires. True love is in
twilight of dreams which burn
like embers in our seething
emotions. Time holds love
eternal and, in every moment,
love will bind us evermore. The
will of our journey is at our feet
when we walk toward love with
willful purity. A candle's eye
watches over the world, as warm
shades of light reveal beauty in
its heavenly form. Dear beloved,
torment our heart, not, for
we are at the mercy of your
will which breaks us into a
thousand pieces. We are a
mosaic of many emotions
and in every fragment,
the vision of beauty in
love never ceases.

Blind Vanity

Humanity was born through
wisdom and brings the light of
truth to human nature. Oh
civilization, the spirit of our
nation has become too firm
with cold-hearted human creatures.
In the walls of time we are born to
live, but only a moment of our
existence. In the depth of our
dreams we seek the universe,

and vanity will make us blind
and inconsistent. The will
to empower is intrinsic to our
character and nature
of our decline. Was
God not created
with pride to
make us feel divine?

Powerless

The human spirit which hungers for power will lose its craving quickly for what it wishes to hold. The heart will harden in blind living and to the world, it will grow cold. The hands of faith will close our eyes as power takes away our sanity which wisdom molds. Power will take hold of us fast and in our delusions, it will turn to gold. A weak spirit will sell its soul to keep power and in arrogance grows bold. We have become slaves to our needs and freedom of spirit to power we have sold.

Light Journey

Oh light, our faraway guest, you have come to tell us your wisdom of what has been and what shall be. Your ever-glowing vision gives

color to all and what you have seen
our feeble eyes longs to see. Will
you touch our awakened soul with
mystical light? In your radiant
beauty, you wash away
the darkness from our sight.
Oh light of wisdom, you bring
back time into our moments
of being. It was in first of time
you set out on your journey,
piercing through the heart
of darkness into the
universe we are
now seeing.

Voice of Morality

Oh, faithful voice of morality, you
have awakened in us the truth of
existence. Will you hold us against
our bodily emotions and help us
from wandering far from our soulful
essence? True virtue can only come
into being once we humble ourselves
to our humanity. Live simply in
worldly needs and wisdom will wash
clean the pride in vanity. Will we
walk into our faith with no
guilt in mind? We search
for happiness which is
everywhere but
still hard to find.

Human Folly

The sound of distant laughter fans
the flame of human folly. Listen not
to the words of human emotions, but to
reason's true calling. In the silence of
our hearts, we can hear the music of
our souls. How deep is our thirst for
water as we see our fate in our bowl?
Will we burn to ground the wealth
of this world and walk toward
our spiritual needs? Were
we not told that the
soul will grow with
poverty and with
time life will
suffer and
bleed?

Wisdom in Truth

Great thoughts escape through
the web of consciousness to become
the substance of human creation.
Will the creative mind capture
their elusive form before they
melt into our imagination?
The will to knowledge is the
spark of curiosity which
moves us to ponder upon
the universe. The fatal
flaw is pride in our
intelligence which
makes simple
wisdom an
intellectual
curse.

∞∞∞∞∞

The weight of our words
will fall to the ground when
we don't think through them
with careful thought. If we
unburden our consciousness,
uplift our wisdom, then our
words will never become
tangled in knots. Speak into
silent wisdom and words
less spoken will set the
mind free. Will we walk
away from the hard reality
and open our eyes
to light our spirit
longs to see?

∞∞∞∞∞

Let There Be Wisdom in Truth

Love flows like an ageless river which longs to meet the great ocean. The human spirit moves toward the boundless soul with love and deep devotion. We journey through life, walk the far-reaching path through endless time to come back home to rest. We are born to live, and live we must with time given, as worldly guests.

∞∞∞∞∞

Silent lips hold nature's beauty, breathe in the splendor of life to give us the peace of love's existence. Words that escape through a lover's heart gives poetry its life-giving substance. A spirit which touches the soul of nature lives in the pure light of heaven. How blessed is the soul that is loved, there is no greater gift to man which was ever given.

∞∞∞∞∞

Let There Be Wisdom in Truth

How will time measure
our beginning and end when
conscious living only lets
us live for the moment?
The human spirit will
forget time as it moves
in seamless movement.
Will we walk with eyes
open and listen to the
steps which lift our
feet? A journey through
time is for young and
old and only achieves
wisdom when fate
and destiny
finally meet.

∞∞∞∞

A fire burns in the human
spirit and keeps the light
of wisdom glowing in the
heart. We are born into
life and the soul of existence
grows with humanity
from the start.

∞∞∞∞

A journey through life will
take us onto the road far
and near. Those afraid of
hardship will not take
their first step toward
life in fear. Life is like
the passing wind and we
live and die in our
short-lived moments.
Time is ever so moving,
there is no time in

reminiscing of
time lost and
wasted
in lament.

∞∞∞∞

A window to our soul is
a glass reality which reflects
in our eyes and breaking it
would shatter all hope in the oneness
of existence. We are the shadow in
our form, and light comes into our
loving vision to become life's only
substance. Will we sense the purity
of nature's mystical fragrance
and hold it in our heart
for all eternity? The voice
of time echoes back our
youthful laughter which
was once the music
of our soulful
serenity.

∞∞∞∞

Blindness only sees the love
that is poured into our souls.
Bewildered eyes search for
meaning which reflects on the
surface of a poor man's bowl.
The mind has willed the hand to
write the words which voice the
music of a mystic poet. Oh,
wandering mystic, your heart
is full of love, but who
among us truly seems
to know it?

∞∞∞∞

The footsteps of reality are
etched in consciousness and
move us to walk deep into
the well of existence. Can
we loosen the will of the
mind and take the small steps
in life's long-distance? We
are like the wind journeying
through the limits of space in
search of purpose and meaning.
Are there any moments left for
conscious reflection in a
soul still lost in
dreaming?

∞∞∞∞

A river of dark clouds walks
silently under the nightly sky.
The mystical wind moves
swiftly through the valley
to hear the great heave in
mountain's pride.
The stars cluster in
warm twilight and keep
vigil over worldly dreams.
The moonlight shimmers
on the moving
surface of a river
paving white light
on the silky stream.

∞∞∞∞

The face of humanity changes
with time, like a river which
branches into the landscape
of earthly reality. Moving
through endless time, lived
life is the will to be. How

Let There Be Wisdom in Truth

deep is our thirst for water
which makes us wonder
how to hold it in our hands?
The mind is drowned in
shallow consciousness
and the wisdom of
non-existence
man will not
understand.

∞∞∞∞∞

The soul of happiness is to lighten
our worldly burden and walk with the
rhythm in our feet. True love is a
river which moves toward the ocean
where two hearts meet. The joy in
living is to breathe in deep the
conscious breath and hold
it close to our human spirit.
The riches of the world
will make us poor and
spiritual suffering
is all that we
will inherit.

∞∞∞∞∞

A freed spirit can hold the
will to write, but it is the
mind which will move the
hand. A pen writes the
words which search for
meaning, but it is our
conscious perception that
seeks to understand. The
truth of wisdom gets written
on empty pages dipped in
pen and ink. A Sufi poet
holds her words

silent and erases
her will to think.

∞∞∞∞

Who can hold the cup of desire and
drink his spirit pure? Oh, Saki, this
drunkenness has taken us in too deep
and we can drink it no more. The
soul is intoxicated with love
of self, and the blood of
humanity spills with every
cup. Oh Saki, what is
heaven? What is hell?
Which one is down?
Which one is up?

∞∞∞∞

Eternal is the truth which drowns
human consciousness and what dies
is the pride of a human being human.
The edges of reality have no
boundaries and the light gives no
form to man or woman. Moral virtue
walks in quiet steps and silent are
words of wisdom, pressed under our
lips. Our existence has become
the shadow in our dreams,
the body in soul and
soul in body totally
eclipsed.

∞∞∞∞

A heart becomes a prisoner
to love and lives in the beauty
of nature. The mystical
scent lifts into the wind
as flowers give it to every
creature. Passion burns

the forest and grows in
and out under the breath
of nature's desires. Who
will pour water on these
burning emotions
and who will put
out the fire?

∞∞∞∞∞

A harsh voice is often heard
but can't silence the moral truth in
our spirit. The power of words
moves the masses and holds true
when the soul hears it. A mind
that thinks and learns simple
wisdom will make no sound.
Words that are heavy with
doubts quickly fall
to the ground.

∞∞∞∞∞

A lush breeze walks through
our window and touches
the spirit with warm emotions.
Nature whispers to the heart
to open the door and welcome
love with humble devotion. The
branches of a tree bathe in the
golden sunshine and flaming
leaves flirt with reality in
shadow and light. The
glorious colors spread
out into the world and
nature becomes
most elegant
to the sight.

∞∞∞∞∞

The wind was born with a
breath of eternity. Love
of nature is the heart of
infinity. The splendor
of life is the essence of
human form. Will we
ever feel the moment
and give joy to life
its mystical
charm?

∞∞∞∞

If we forgot ourselves, then how will
we know ourselves in the mirror of
self-reflection? Those who lose their
beginning and move toward their
end will have no purpose, no
direction. Will we break the glass of
our existence which no longer
reflects the light of what we want to
see? The wholeness of life lay
wasted in time of what
we were and what
we come to be.

∞∞∞∞

A wandering fakir begs for
salvation, singing the mystical song
that voices the truth of life's
wisdom. Will we open our soul and
walk into that which houses our
spiritual kingdom? The riches of the
world make us poor when we waste
our lives chasing the wind. Listen
to the words of a fakir who
unhinges our heart,
and awakens
our mind.

∞∞∞∞

Let There Be Wisdom in Truth

A great secret to knowledge is to master the art of ignorance. We can never achieve intelligence if we flaunt our knowledge with arrogance. Do we not know that the truth we seek is not written in any book? Curiosity will open our eyes, but it is the mind which must give it a modest look.

∞∞∞∞

A curious mind burns with passion and will look for light in truth. The vision of nature's beauty is imbued in our soul and becomes the lifeblood of our youth. Eyes open into conscious reality and see the world in all its wonder. How immense are the mysteries of life, the mind sits silently and ponders?

∞∞∞∞

Love Beyond

In smoke-filled dreams, the embers of desire burn into the night. It is the vision of reality which drifts deep into our conscious soul. The graceful hand of the wind spreads our existence far into the world. Time will lift the spirit and the fulfillment of joy empties into our consciousness. Happiness is the blood of humanity, but it is the sorrows of the world which bleeds into our nature. The human spirit is weary and searches for beauty that bewilders its wandering vision. Are we awake or truly sleeping in our dreams when consciousness opens our eyes? The beauty of nature is our deep comfort, and mystical to a poet who understands the splendor of its creation.

Oh, Hafiz, she has become the destiny of our existence, the master of our will. Love is the will and act of tender benevolence. Love is all-knowing and infinite in mystical sentiments. Oh, Hafiz, words of love purse our lips, but it is their silence which tangles us in knots. The melody of music is the rhythm of love. The mind of a Sufi mystic holds love in spiritual form which emanates with everlasting joy. Can true love ever be found in a world blind in self-absorption? Why love an image which holds no light, no vision? True love is beyond

reason, beyond comprehension. True
love is the hand which holds us close
to our heart. True love is born when
the soul gives up its bodily form.
A light which washes the surface
of reality gives love its infinite glow.
It is the veil under conscious
existence which hides the divine
nature of love. The essence of love is
the seed which grows roots in our
spirit. Love is not a flower but the
fragrance which is held captive by
the gentle breeze. True love is never
holy until it is purified in the
sacred river of nonexistence. Oh
Hafiz, our spirit has become dense,
and yet the power to love lifts
us high to touch the sky.

The mold of humanity is the divine
love for creation. The breath of our
existence is the love for life. Love is
an all-consuming state which binds
us to the universe and gives unity to
mind, body, and spirit. A river flows
through us and moves deeper
and deeper into our soul. The
edges of reality fade into
the vastness of our mind.
Oh Hafiz, we are all
wanderers in search
of true love which our
dreams long to
seek but
can't find.

Coming of Spring

The majestic mountains give birth to raging rivers which cut through the landscape of nature's heart. Trees hold firm in their rooted existence as they lie frozen in their unmoved state. The fast-paced wind blows over mountain peaks as virgin snow blankets the rugged face of hard reality. Deep winter frost lies heavy upon the forest. All living forms are under the mercy of winter's bitter tyranny and feel the burden they hope to overcome. The ever-white snow hides the footsteps of time as the will of life is buried in unbroken silence. Nature's beauty sleeps, hibernates from the eyes of the world.

Harsh nights hold us prisoners in our homes until the warm sunlight gives us the courage to open our doors. The high-reaching mountain peaks cut into the glistening blue sky as clouds walk like pilgrims giving homage to nature's holy relics. The evergreen trees stand bold postured in their steep climb, sloped, and aligned in their footsteps. Distant valleys glimmer like sparkling jewels on the ground as smoke rises from rooftop chimneys. Winter's hold on nature's soul is strong, but the great warmth of the radiant sun melts it all away. It is the voice of spring which awakens the seeds of reality. Rivers run

to tell the world the coming
of spring is in the air. The
lush green meadows throw
off their winter coat and
nature's eye awakens
to colors of life:
here, there, and
everywhere.

All Eternity

The night falls heavily upon our
breath. Darkness is born through life
and death. The stars sparkle in
their glory, burning their light
for all eternity. Twilight holds the
world in a mystical dream as the
conscious mind surrenders its
serenity. The eyes of reality
wander through ever-expanding
dreams. Life is like a river,
slow-moving, flowing
deep into our
conscious
stream.

Colors of Life

Oh beloved, into my soul you
have entered like a slow
moving summer breeze. You
are the flower of nature which

gives my spirit the colors of life. The
sorrow of living is no longer my
burden when your laughter lightens
the heart in strife. In my light,
you have become the beauty
of my loving form.
The sound of your voice
moves the heartfelt emotions
and makes the soul calm
with ease. You are the
purity of God's simple
truth which my world
looks for and
only sees.

Sacred Creed

Justice is the sacred creed that binds
morality to the masses. The eternal
laws hold firm their character and
keep a light on wisdom as time
passes. Humans walk toward
humanity like a river bending
toward the oceans. How far will
life go seeking their fill of human
emotions? Moral virtue is sacred and
will remain divine in our humble
soul. Will we know the way to
truth which will bind us
to our spiritual role?

Seeking Pleasures

Seek full pleasure in life until
pleasures hold no further joy. To

live under the grace of humility
is the only character humanity
wills to destroy. Wisdom bleeds
our spirit when pride cuts into
our fragile existence. Why hoard
the treasure of the world only
to empty the spirit of its essence.
Who among us has not cried
in the moment of being
born? We are born, we
live and we die; what
is there then
to mourn?

Walk Softly

Moonlight paves the way,
draws our steps to walk softly
and silently toward the light. In
the darkness of night, the spirit
wanders freely under the veil
of sight. The world slumbers
from the ever-tiring burden
of working in time. The rungs
of the ladder from Earth to Heaven
are under our feet but get harder
to climb. The stars burn
like candles, drip, drip and
drip into our conscious
dreams. What will we be
when we are awakened
from our broken, tattered
reality which remains
torn at the
seams?

True Self

True Self is an illusion one creates in the conscious realization of oneself. How do we find the Self in worldly reality when knowledge of who we are holds no wisdom, no truth? Like a shadow which holds light, the Self is bound to the spirit of our being. Was it the true Self which gave us the real purpose of God's creation? The Self is the heart of morality which guides our steps in life's journey. In the stillness of time, the mind is ever moving around the Self for real understanding. The will of our soul brings the Self into light, into form. Life is a never-ending struggle to know the Self. Love of Self will liberate us from our mind, body, and spirit.

The heaviness of earthly existence holds the Self above ground. Will we take in the vision of wisdom and give life its light in truth? The Self is within, and the Self is without. We become nonexistent and yet exist in all of existence. In the metamorphosis of our conscious existence, the mind transforms into the Self and the Self transforms into the mind. The universe is whole with our imagination and the Self is consumed in the wholeness of eternal reality. The Self is divine

nature which molds the spirit
into our being. The joy in our
nature is the all-fulfilling
Self which will satiate the
emptiness of our needs.

The great love of Self emanates with
beauty and colors which become the
fulcrum of meaningful existence.
The gift of life is sacred which the
true Self sees with every passing
moment. The hardship of life is self-
willed only when we can't let go of
ourselves. The pleasures of the
world are self-giving only when we
let go of our desires. The thirst for
salvation is self-realization only
when we are satisfied with
what we have.

The breath of wisdom is self-
fulfilling only when we breathe in
our conscious awareness. A mind
is self-liberating only when it gives
itself to freedom of thought. The
mirror is self-reflecting only when
we look at ourselves with naked
eyes. If we become self-conscious
of the great Self then the fragments
of our human nature becomes whole.
The world is a mosaic of timely
existence which the true
Self needs to satisfy
its spiritual role.

LET THERE BE WISDOM IN TRUTH

Love is like a river that seeks the great ocean

In Love

Will you give us one night in eternity to love? The wings of life have touched the sky. Love is like a river that seeks the great ocean. Waves of emotions long for the sandy shore to be absorbed in the oneness of love. Oh Kabir, we taste our thirst in wine which you pour into our soul. We ferment in the sweet water of our existence, and the blood of humanity comes to surface with joy. Intoxicated in the ecstasy of love, the mind erases all limits in our reality. Divine is the vision of love which is all-seeing and all-embracing.

Divine is the love which God breathes into our spirit. Divine is the light which brings colors into our eyes. Divine is the truth which wisdom gives us with worldly compassion. Will we find tranquility in moments of time and grow old with grace in our age full existence? Divine is God's affections when we give our heart to those we love. Divine is God's mercy when we show kindness to those who do us wrong. The nightly stars burn with passion and touch our eyes with their mystical glow. Will we open our hearts to the oneness of love? Will we give up the world to seek true love? Will we carry the empty bowl to fill love with abundance? Will we

touch the red-hot embers of fire and
not be afraid of being burned? The
essence of love is the fragrance
which gives life to the empty soul.

The beauty of love is written in
amorous words which poets voice
with eloquence. To love oneself is to
love all and to love all is what makes
love great. Will we become the
vision of this world and spread the
colors of love to eyes which no
longer see? A pearl of luminous
wisdom comes from the summer
breeze; we must let love enter our
hearts and never let it walk away.
Will we open our door and let the
guest from heaven come into our
spirit? In the eyes of a lover's dream,
the world sleeps quietly and is all-
encompassing. The dawn of day
awakens with the sweet honeyed
scent of earthly flowers as the
warm simmering emotions
rise from our spirit.

The rustic light of the golden sun
comforts our soul. Is love not the
thirst for existence which clings like
dewdrops on the body of budding
roses? Love's everlasting vigor
never fades, never dies.
A candle's light gives love its
sensuous form and glows with
beauty for the world to see.
Like a river which flows into
the ocean, love moves toward
the great spirit of humanity.

Like a forest which veils the
virgin soul of nature, love
will veil the purity of our
spiritual form. The serenity
of love is when two souls
become one to quell
their emotional
storm.

Tangled Form

The web of conscious existence
spreads into reality and traps
the soul into its tangled form.
Did we not fall foot-deep into a
weather-beaten life and get
caught in our naked storm?
The well of needs reflects
no light as we look into it with
our curious face. Will we pull
ourselves up with our own
will and humble our pride with
grace? The eyes of perception move
through our minds and cuts
through our freedom. The illusion
of dreams has no walls and
keeps the doors opened
to our wisdom.

Walk the Part

Truth brings us to awareness and
unravels man's greatest lies.
Time will not lament the wastes
of humanity or whether the body
lives or dies. Silently we walk under
the vastness of the ever-expanding
world hoping to keep still the
restless heart. The journey
through the Self is endless, but
we must convince our souls to walk
the part. We are destined to move
toward our end the day we open our
eyes to consciousness. We are
caught in the trap of existence and
the strings of reality keep pulling us
back into our madness. Will we ever
overcome life and come home to rest
with ease? Why chase the wind
when we can sit in
peace and enjoy
the elusive
breeze?

Dust of Reality

A tree falls under the gravity of time
and the forest awakens into the
conscious moment. In purity
of creation, nature gives us the
flowers of the world, but in the
envious hands of humanity, there is
no atonement. The veil of beauty is
what makes the eyes go blind

in love. The mirror of our eyes
reflects the splendor of heaven given
to us from above. We will one day
become the dust of reality to be
swept away by a gust of strong
wind. The dreams of the nights
will continue to burn, and
the embers of forgotten
memories will
remain for others
to find.

Autumn Breeze

Glazed in the frost of autumn,
the moonlight blankets the
naked trees. Rusty brown
leaves cling to their mother's
breast plucked by the cold
hand of the autumn breeze.
The gray-silver clouds move
silently over the dark sky.
In strong branched trees
the owl sits still and searches
for prey with a wild look in
her eye. Oh Night, you linger
in your darkness, smoldering
in the dreamy reflection of
twilight. The stars hold
the essence of light
as humanity
sleeps under
the stillness
of night.

Morning Light

A crow breaks the silence of
morning light and sits on a
branch in his black silhouette
with posing laughter. The autumn
breeze has picked up the pace
and the pulse of emotions moves
nature a little faster. The rustic
orange-brown leaves scattered
on the ground move hither, thither
in rustling sounds by the moving

wind. Trees rooted to the ground are silent and stare stoically at the world from the front and behind. The shadow of reality moves closer and closer into bodily form seeking more light. The day reflects the soul of nature, everlasting joy, and majestic in sight.

Moving River

A river moves in mystical ways under the cresting waves of silky water. Virgin snow melts in the warmth of spring and brings life into her. The wind's gentle hand stirs nature's emotions and steals the fragrance of budding roses. The thirst for life is soaked in heavenly rains as trees stand firm in humble poses. Great mountains with majestic faces grow to touch the sky. Heaven and earth are lost lovers, their separation makes the dewdrops cry. Out in the open field, the crows give a call to spring to come into dawn's light. The golden sun awakens the evergreen forest and washes away the bitter pain of winter's bite.

Never-ending

A cup holds water for life but to drink we first must give up our thirst. Human dignity is to hold moral ground, but we must walk through our conscious will first. Will humanity ever give up its pride in being human and move toward light in humble ways? The hand of reality molds our spirit; time will give us our nights and days. The never-ending hunger for self-realization will starve human passion forevermore. Where are the boundaries between inner and outer reality when human consciousness closes our doors? The eyes of human existence hold too much light, and wisdom becomes our moral truth. The dust of time becomes fragments of humanity that settles like sediments into conscious youth.

Beauty of Nature

Oh beauty of Nature, the mystical vision of reality has become the landscape of your dreams. How you flirt with our eyes is the secret of your charm. The colors of the world are hidden in your soul. Deep spirited is poetry which is written in your praise. It is your divine perfection which is pure and untouched. Imbued in your desires are the burning emotions of true love, fanned by the sensuous breeze. Humanity reflects in the harmony of your nature and the human soul is deep-rooted in your heart. A never-ending forest vast as the ocean keeps hidden the beauty of Nature from our envious eyes. The wind moves in silent wonder to open the doors to Nature's spirit. Rivers move under her feet and the cold mist lifts toward the spacious blue sky.

Leaves rustle with a symphony of sound as the glorious sun brings her to light. A bed of ivory snow covers her bodly form. Deep-seated is Nature's love, the seeds of all wisdom. Oh Nature, your vision of reality is heaven on earth. Your spiritual truth is the lifeblood of human existence. You are the face of unspoken poetry which can't be written. You are a vision of our inner eye which can't see anything more. You hold time still as you embrace us with motherly devotion. You cleanse our spirit and wash away the stains of our humanity. You humble our senses and give our minds the depth of perception. You quench our thirst for life and nourish our spirit with your infinite grace.

Oh Nature, humanity tears you naked and ravages your beauty with unforgiving hands. We burn your forest for our selfish needs. We take away your delicate flowers with our strong-willed desires. We are the guilty souls which you forgive with kindness and humility. Oh Nature, you take away our empty existence the moment you come into our soul. Our spirit is liberated the moment we walk into your world. We forget our human suffering the moment we hear the music of your world. The spirit of purpose sleeps in your arms as you hold us in your dreams. In the dark shades of Nature's mystery, the full moon holds vigil over the world. Stars burn bright in the nightly sky and keep their eyes open til dawn's light.

Mountains stand broad and tall in their glory as they watch over you with guarded devotion. Oh Nature, the fragrance of spring is upon your earthly breath. Dewdrops fall from blades of grass, tears of rapture in first of dawn. It is your sacred call which lifts the

butterflies into the wind. On the hills,
in the valleys, your voice moves
through the air in a continuous
melody of sound. Oh Nature, we
are bound to you with our mind and
spirit. Your unrivaled beauty is the
vision for soul of being. The richness
in your colors is a miracle
which lives in our eyes. The
ever wanting of you is
all-consuming,
eternal, and
never dies.

Let There Be Wisdom in Truth

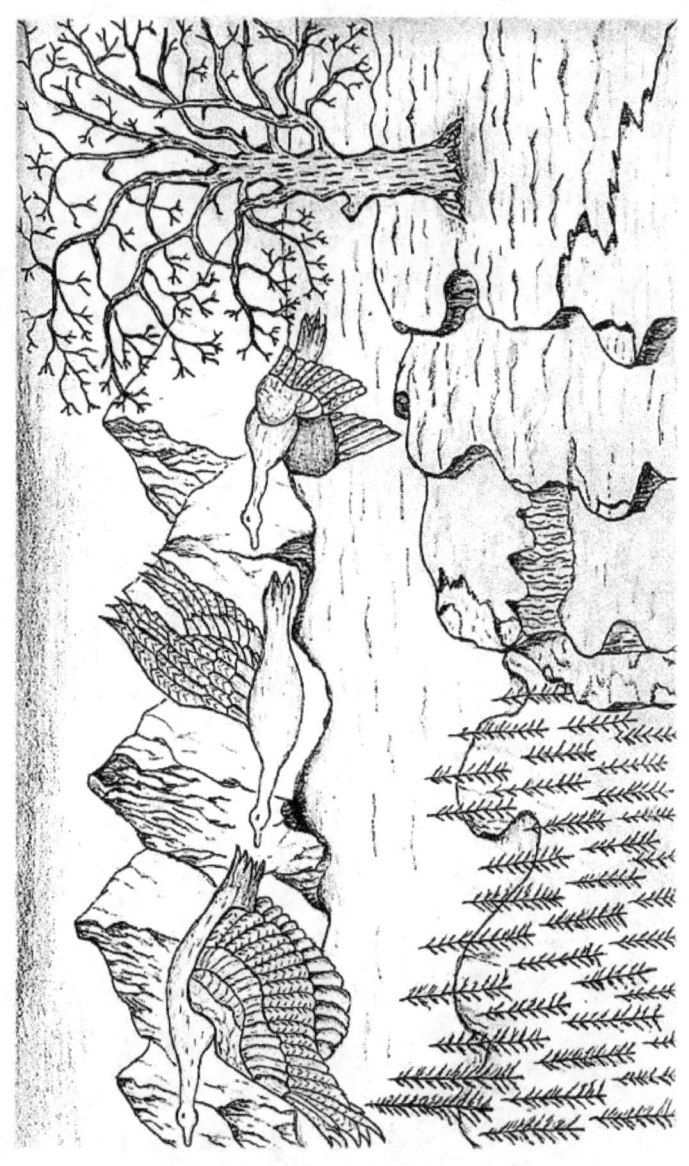

Soul of Nature

Will the spirit be moved by the beauty of nature as colors touch our conscious soul? The wind holds the scent of life, a sensuous fragrance of being young. The purity of love flows in nature's heart and the blood of humanity bleeds for more. The sun awakens into day unveiling the light of the world before our eyes. Open blue sky, deep as the ocean, reflects the soul of nature's mysteries. The river's surface reflects our emotions as thoughts move like waves through our reflective mind.

The timeless trees, frozen in their state are the soldiers, the guardians of nature's blessed landscape. Their total love and devotion embrace the voice of nature's call. A sea of daffodils dances in the wind and nature's eye can see them all. Rustling leaves break their silence and jubilation of sound rises through the wind and settles in nature's soul. Subdued clouds, pale and gray, walk across the horizon, endlessly moving through the vast open sky. Birds take flight in search of harmony in new found freedom. Flowers open their colors to the world, a vision of reality painted by nature's sweeping brush of emotions. A mosaic of beauty in fragments of truth, nature will hold our passions, and bring unity to our

senses. Engraved in our soul is the
spirit of nature's mystical love.
Pearls of dewdrops fall from
parted leaves to touch the
lips of thirst-filled roses.

Mountains soaring into the sky give us
the courage to reach their peaks. Rivers
move silently into our conscious
minds and flow into our wandering
dreams. A forest which blankets the
earth gives comfort and a home to all
living souls. Oh nature, you have
moved the spirit and touched
our hearts to love once more.
We hold time in our hands of
wisdom as all of creation
walks through
your door.

Moon Flower

The moonflower awakens into
the ivory glow of night. The black
charcoal sky drowns her beauty in
the purity of gray-silver twilight.
The world sleeps in its mystical
dreams. A mist blankets the forest as
nature keeps vigil over creation, so it
seems. The veil of truth holds love
captive in the soul of a wandering
mystic. The fragrance of nature
holds the wind as the beauty
of reality becomes
seductive and
holistic.

Coming of Rain

Life-giving is the coming of rain as Spring melts away Winter's bitter and icy tears. Heavenly rains are warm, and the soul is immersed in the purity of water to wash away worldly existence with no fear. A subtle breeze stirs laughter in rustling leaves. The splendor of sunlight awakens nature's beauty in the breath of creation as it breathes and heaves. A river moves toward the edge of night as the streams of water reflects in the moon's gleam. Are the coming rains also the coming of life as the world grows from the seeds of nature's mystic dream?

Moral Ground

A woeful voice of wisdom is heard too late as the heart laments the lost soul of a child in man. Will humanity ever learn from their history of destruction and not be consumed in flames they fan? Did we forget that we are guests in our moments of existence, here today, gone tomorrow? The rich will hoard their wealth, but the poor will give it away with no sorrow. Those who no longer walk on the moral

ground are afraid to come out
of their doors. The voice
of reason has been silenced
as sounds of mocking
laughter sour.

True Love

It is with true love that we
will find real meaning in life's
existence. Will we humble our
soul to the one we love with all
our essence? The purity of love
is beyond beauty and remains
evergreen. We will remain in
love forever if we keep love
serene. Love only comes once,
and thereafter no true love
will ever come around. If
we lose it to the world, then
we will search, but true
love will never
be found.

All-Knowing

The fragments of reality
gave birth to the wholeness of
perception which cuts through
the consciousness of self-expression.
To seek that which seeks us is the
intellectual landscape of man's one

true obsession. Like a candle which burns in the world of reality, our spirit will glow with novelty of existence. How far will we journey into our creative imagination to realize that our will can't cover infinite distance? What is a mind to the thought of seeking, but searching the light of truth that is all-knowing. Are we not a mosaic in broken time, moving deeper and deeper into wisdom to collect the fragments of knowledge which are ever-growing?

Let There Be Wisdom in Truth

Breath of Love

The vastness of our being has moved us farther apart and yet in reminiscence, we have become so close. The gentle wind whispers your name and we listen to your voice in untold wonder. The breath of love is the air which holds you in. It is the fragrance of your body which holds your tenderness in our sensuous dreams. Like a delicate red rose, your lips are pressed upon your face with love of form. In your eyes, the vision of our deep spirit reflects the divine light. A fire burns in the water of our thirst, and our thirst for each other can never put out the fire.

We are born in the shadow of each other's light. What we have promised we will keep, but what we keep is no solace to your sacred soul. Hope for love brews in our hearts; it will not drown you in our deepest ocean. In the dimness of our broken existence, our eyes still see the oneness of your reality. It is the night, the mystical night which takes us into time. Our bewildering eyes are entrenched in longing and search for you between heaven and earth. To suffer is the path to wisdom, but love consumes all suffering. Wandering emotions become the soul of passion and in love they have found a home.

Let There Be Wisdom in Truth

Oh beloved, the whole of existence came into being first when we looked into each other's eyes. Will we ever find you in words which have escaped our mind? Is pleasure not a mixture of joy and grief, the fate of life which we seek to live? A candle's vigil is hope in waiting for two souls to become one. In stillness of time, love becomes eternal, and the spirit glows, seeking the eternal light. Why does love grow precious once it moves farther away with time? It is the fear of losing love which makes love more divine.

Broken love is like a withering leaf, drifting into the wind, lost to the soul which loved it most. Love will never grow old; the vigor of emotions will forever keep it young in spirit. A journey through love will never come to an end until two outreaching hands touch. Oh beloved, your love is our everlasting dream, and the soul of our existence as such.

Mosaic of Truth

Humanity can't see darkness for they have been blinded by light. Will we ever listen to the voice of truth which can't silence our ears? Watered-down wisdom will not wash away the illusions of reality. The revelation of truth speaks to our spirit and keeps us moving toward the moral path. The hands which shape the clay of our substance will not maintain our spirit. The will which moves our body is too heavy for the mind to bring to consciousness. Why anchor our soul to time when seeking wisdom in truth will free us from ignorance.

Human nature is the face of humanity when it looks in the mirror of self-reflection. The whole of man's existence is a mosaic of broken dreams. Truth falls into our awareness and the mind will pick it up with conscious will. The truth of our being becomes the seeds of possibilities and the fruit of our effort. Lifted by the wind is the dust of time which uncovers the layers of our buried truth.

Stagnation holds us still, but the mind is ever-moving and seeks truth in clarity of thought. What will we see when the light of reason lifts the veil from our darkness? We know not what we need to know,

Let There Be Wisdom in Truth

and seeking to know that
which cannot be
known and that
is human
arrogance.

Let There Be Wisdom in Truth

Molded by the hands of faith, and shaped by the will of God, the human spirit walks through time seeking the soul of its being.

Oh, Lord

Oh Lord, you are the end and beginning of all existence. Oh, Lord! In your spirit exists the great light of wisdom. You are the infinite and the sum of all fragments of reality are one with your wholeness. Day and night obey your will and time bends at both ends under the power of your touch. In deep prayers, the grace of your ever-presence gives substance to our spirit. With every breath, we breathe in your love and breathe out the purity of your perfection.

Our shallowness can never reach your depth and yet you pour into our souls your deepest wisdom. We live through your existence and by knowing your world we come to know ourselves evermore. The universal truth is revealed to us in prayers. Our hands are folded, and we ask for your humility and guidance in our human ways. You are the king of all kings and your judgment is the final word. In the simplest of things, you remain simple and the most complex you make so simple. Your infinite is never reachable, but you still touch us with your infinite soul. Your vast knowledge humbles us in our ignorance. Molded by the hands of faith and shaped by the will of God, the human spirit walks through time, seeking the soul of its being. Limitless is your truth which goes

beyond our limits. We are a speck of
nothingness and yet you give
everything through this nothingness.
Oh Lord, give us moral courage to
see beyond ourselves. We are weak
in mind and our spirit has become
too worldly. Give us direction to
fulfill our role in our momentary
life. It was in your great love
that you created Man. Help
us rid the flames of
hatred that too
often evil fans.

Rustic Face

Memories scatter into the wind,
swept away by the withered leaves
of time. Oh, fading of youthful
dreams, you remain eternally subtle
in colors sublime. Time will reveal
the aged lines of wisdom
in our rustic faces. The mirrors of
reality reflect our weathered
existence, time etched in worldly
traces. The love we hold in our heart
is our only face, moldedin beauty
by creation. We see our rustic
face in mirrors of self-reflection
as we move through time
to live and die in
life's binding
obligations.

Righteousness

If equality, justice, and true happiness truly exists, then why do wars, hatred, and evil persist? It is human nature which makes what's right wrong and what's wrong right which we can't resist. We live in our circular world and run around blindly chasing the tail of greed. Why dig our graves deep when we are already buried in the shallowness of our needs? Only with conscious awareness can moral virtue bring wisdom to sight. The guilt of humanity makes us human, but it is love for righteousness which surrenders darkness to light.

A Pebble of Reality

Many days and nights our steps have walked the narrow and darkened road. Our eyes have looked at slow-moving time, as age deepens the burden which wisdom unloads. In the niches of our dreams, we erase the essence of our human feature. The mind unveils the face of reality and the spirit can't see through the opacity

of its nature. A pebble
of reality is released from
the hand and moves the
surface under the stillness
of a pond. Waves of
conscious emotions
move the soul onto
the shore and
beyond.

Light of Wisdom

A life lived in ignorance is painful
and long. A mind grows in light
of reason and holds onto wisdom
strong. Will we wash the guilt
of humanity with the blood of our
spirit? The nature of existence is the
great miracle of God we inherit.
Why do we seek empty dreams
which are not worth seeking?
Let them go. Why should a child
grow into the man only to
become blind to the
world he knows?

Firm Ground

Truth only exists when it rests on
conscious reality and settles on the
vision of our inner light. The
branches of a tree spread far and

Let There Be Wisdom in Truth

wide, only to come back to their
roots of what nature holds in sight.
Morality grows sturdy with time
only when wisdom is held on
firm ground. Human virtue is
the voice of humanity that makes
life profound. We are born
into our conscious spirit
which brings us back to the
center of our being. How
can we know the truth
when we no longer
hold the vision of
what we are
seeing?

Simple Life

The wealth of spirit is the health of our soul. It is our only comfort in life which we should drink daily from our sacred bowl. How essential is the lifeblood of existence is only realized when we become deathly sick. Be good to others, do no harm, and live life simply; that is the trick. We become fragmented in our needs and the well of water is too heavy for our thirst. How can we live in peace when the humble ways of living we have cursed?

Mystified

In a journey through life, we will walk with heaviness in our boots. Time grows into the soul and takes us back to our roots. Will we open our eyes into the soul of nature and give up our human pride? The beauty of the world will lift our spirit and the mind will awaken totally mystified. Live for the moment and consciousness will take us deep into our thoughts. Why do we keep turning and twisting in the web of reality and tie ourselves in knots?

Web of Vanity

We hide in the walls of our homes
and the shadow of our spirit has
found its resting place. The heart
of soul will not open its doors
to the world and no longer reflect
our welcoming face. Will we tear
the walls which trap our sanity?
Pride will imprison the soul
and there will be no escape
from this web of vanity.
Will we come out of our
darkness and walk into
the world revealed?
My words are silent;
they speak volume
but my lips
are sealed.

Let There Be Wisdom in Truth

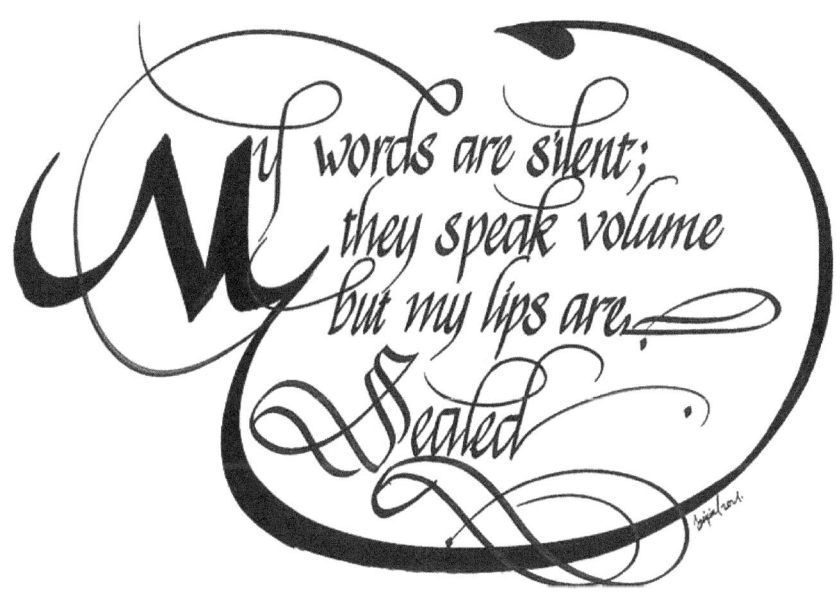

My words are silent;
they speak volume
but my lips are
Sealed

Simplicity

A heart suffers for love in the spirit and the burden of suffering lifts the human soul toward wisdom. It is the heavy footsteps into reality which lighten the mind. The hardship of our journey makes the human will stronger. Only when we walk into darkness can we face fear with courage and dignity. Will we listen to our laughter which mocks our shallow existence? Will we see the wealth in poverty which lightens the load in life? Live simple and spend time relishing the subtle beauty of conscious existence. Can we give vision to our dreams and open the mind to simplicity of being alive? A spirit which lives through suffering will hold every moment and in wisdom will thrive.

Being Human

Man is driven to act through the will of his conviction. Delusions of grandeur are deep-rooted in his human nature. What is reality is no longer real and what one sees is no longer reality. Hypocrisy splits humanity in two, one forms consciousness, and the other forms blind vanity. The stench of moral decay is the breath of humanity. The art of being righteous is the act of self-deception. The noble spirit mocks human chivalry as self-serving and destructive. Once we sell our souls to power and wealth, we will never get back our happiness. The will of humanity is the will of God. Light spreads into our soul and darkness reveals the nature of being human. If death is in every step of life, then the fear of dying becomes our conscious struggle to live. Humanity builds only to destroy, and time will lay waste all that we build. It is the savage sword of human nature that spills the blood of God's creation.

Human history is written on battlefields and through destruction, the birth of collective consciousness spills into the heart of humanity. Have we become martyrs in the folly of human tragedy? How do we liberate the human spirit from our tortured past? Is the illusion of being free a trap for our need to be free? Dead souls are bought by those who have no soul. Once humanity sells their soul, they become slave masters to evil that bears no grace. Thirst of man is the deep well of sorrow. We hunger for self-realization and yet it is our fate to be human that starves us even more.

Wealth and power blind the weak spirit and leaves them poor and powerless with time. Simple wisdom keeps our eyes fixed to reality and gives us the richness of life's simple truth. The body is a prisoner of soul, but it is the perception of being that opens the doors. To escape from the will of power, we must break through the walls of human existence. The human spirit grows with wisdom and takes in the fortunes of perception with every breath. We have become the infinite within our being, a shadow within shadow, and our duality is the bridge between life and death.

Conscious Moment

A conscious moment of our existence is time eternal. The residues of our mind are layered in our thoughts. The perception of Self is what we perceive in our consciousness. In the face of humanity, the eyes will reflect our human emotions. The power of will is the courage which will move us beyond time. The hands of fortune hold us in our hearts. The search for true love is hidden in our souls. The light of wisdom reveals the darkness of our fears. Blind is the truth of humanity which man wishes not to see. The labor of our existence is to walk into the world fully formed.

There is no respite for the weary spirit when chasing dreams is all-consuming. The shadow loses its form when light of reason is fully realized. A river of knowledge is the ever-changing surface of water which can't hold time. A mind becomes deeper than the ocean when thoughts become heavy in our conscious world. How can human mortality ever come to terms with the infinity of time? The human spirit has become the enigma to self-realization. In every moment of time, the layers of experience become the remains of our nights and days. A child is born in the purity of life only to be led astray by the hands of the world. The seeds of our being grow above the surface of reality and nurtured in love make us spiritually strong. The wind whispers our name and nature takes us into its beauty to give us the true meaning of love.

Oh youthful laughter, you still come like an echo from our past to kindle forgotten memories written on empty pages of time. Life becomes a whitewashed dream and our mystical light dissolves into our soul. The distant stars touch the spirit, the never-ending glory of life's eternal moments. Will we ever hold still life's steps and ponder on the splendor of nature's vision? The colors of the world are absorbed in our eyes and run into our blood. The road toward life is under the will of mind, and once we move forward then only the footsteps of time are left behind. The pendulum of life swings in two extremes of reality but slowly comes back to the center of our being. Are we not conscious of the river, a drift in time which takes us further into our journey?

Behind Time

The eyes of humanity are under the veil of night and sleep under the soft glow of the moonlight. Dreams lay waste in time as consciousness drifts in and out of self-awareness. Nature's beauty is the grace of eternity and gives us solace in her soul. It is the loving spirit of the wind which moves the world. It is the river which flows through our mind's eye, which forms our mystical vision. Light holds our shadow in form and the heart glows in the warmth of soothing emotions. A candle's glow is most revealing of our non-existing world. The thirst for lost pleasures still lingers in our mind. Memories are the mist in our eyes, racing back in time for what is left behind. Can we taste the sweetness of freedom? Will we escape into our dreams without fear of being lost in our world? If we are awakened into our dreams, then they become the splendor of moments everlasting. Why did we come out of our dreams to bear the burden of this world, the soul keeps asking?

Let There Be Wisdom in Truth

Touch of Love

The voice within will emanate out into the world with words of wisdom. Like a circle with no end, fate will walk us forward to come full circle in life's journey. What path will our steps take when hardship falls upon our world in darkest of ways? Lost in human dance, the world will become glaring in our ever-moving reality. We move into our emotions to feel the warmth and comfort of our existence.

A rose is stripped of its fragrance; the wind's hands are mischievous and innocent to the touch. Nature's eye awakens the soul and beauty holds us prisoner in her charm. The wings of freedom fly deep into our spirit to love life more. Love will come into being only when we remain bound to our existence. Love holds no walls, no distinctions, and will erase all divides in humanity. Love is mystical to the one who loves and divine to the one who surrenders to its will. The vastness of time holds love eternal and never changes its beauty and form. Nature is our vision to love and a beautiful creation in our poetic mind.

Oh beloved, your eyes are the pearls of my world and without your light, darkness is all-encompassing and complete. Sad and hopeless is a

soul which will not open its doors to
love. Lost is the spirit which will not
seek its other half. Wasted is youth
which has not felt the soulful touch
of love. In love, we are born;
through love, we become the
essence of our humanity.
What is love but a spirit
of being in which we
give ourselves to
it with humble
dignity?

Awakened Mind

Will we let go of ourselves and give freedom the wings to soar into the human spirit? Can we liberate our vision into the sweeping blue sky? Oh Humanity, come in and break out of your shell, the hand of eternity knocks at your doors. Freedom is spontaneous, ever-moving, and gives wisdom and elegance to an awakened mind. A voice of reason calls for our soul to give truth to our silent words. Will we free our steps which holds us firm to the ground?

Words which hold no meaning are erased by the mind. A body which holds no hunger makes peace with poverty of existence. Will we walk slowly in rhythm with time and guide our steps to cover great distances? Nature's beauty is sublime to the spirit, which we see with compassion in our eyes. Life is ever-changing and ever-shifting moments in time which take us through our humble journey. Trapped in the web of reality, the conscious will seek escape from worldly dreams. Thoughts of being human is to be human when we think of who and what we truly are. It is the nature of our being which enslaves the soul. It is the pride of being human which remains unbroken. Humanity will grow with time, but the world can no

Let There Be Wisdom in Truth

longer give us wisdom in
our humble existence.

Trapped inside our conscious being,
we will not give up worldly
pleasures to enrich our spirit. Lost
time is never gained, and lost
freedom is never regained. Live
today and grow into tomorrow, the
story of life is our worldly play. We
move into our fate and never realize
how far we have strayed from our
beginning. The conscious eye turns
inward when the world closes
outward. We are born free
and our spirit lives and
dies for freedom.
Human liberty holds no
bondage and becomes
the soul of inner
wisdom.

Web of Dreams

Shattered by the mirror of self-reflection are the broken dreams lost to reality. The collective whole is the light of reason which unveils the blindness of our existence. We will know our humanity if we face the truth with our moral vision. Our eyes are the open window into reality and dreams are the doors to our spiritual being. The truth of the world is held in our spirit. Love of nature's beauty is the creative impulse which brews in conscious dreams. A mind holds our words in abundance with fullness of thought.

The realization of our being awakens us to the voice of our silent soul. Is reality not an illusion, trapped in the web of dreams? The colors of the world give the light its hidden meaning. Consciousness walks between the lines of shadow and form. Time moves mountains toward the sky, but it is our dreams which lay them at our feet. The passion of God's grace is the birth of the human race. The grandness of our dreams is the pride of being human. In the fullness of night, the stars will leave us mystical. In the stillness of time, dreams escape into the mind of human imagination. Freedom of will walks us into our dreams to be forever transformed.

Let There Be Wisdom in Truth

The edges of perception become
the mosaic of dreams which
form whole from our fragments
of existence. It is dreams of
immortality which find us
in our mortality, so it seems.
Dawn's light walks through
our window and touches our
spirit to come out
of our dreams.

Let There Be Wisdom in Truth

Wisdom in Truth

A wandering poet holds no
thoughts in her heart, but
the voice to speak is her
words of loving emotions.
How sweet is the voice of
wisdom as beauty of nature
moves into her soul with
no notion? Oh Nature, were
you not born in a river of
dreams, searching for great
love toward the ocean?
The spirit of poetry escapes
her mind's eye as she
prays for true faith
in devotion.

∞∞∞∞∞

A mind's eye which is blind to
the truth of realization is lost to
civilization. Civility is the heart
of creation which builds strong
nations to bring peace, harmony,
and salvation. The history
of humanity is written in the
spirit of war, and damnation.
How do we overcome
pride, gluttony, desires
and temptation?

∞∞∞∞∞

Words hold no power until
a strong voice speaks them with
firmness in reason. If truth is
sold to lies, then the virtue of
our words have committed
the ultimate treason. Will
the soul ever hold up our

heavy words, laced with
deception? A life with
no clarity is lost to
the world and
will receive no
great reception.

∞∞∞∞

Will you please tell the spirit that
these eyes have become blind and
have seen too much light? Living
without purpose is like walking
aimlessly in the darkness of night.
Will we ever take a moment to open
into the wisdom of our existence?
Wealth of life is a gift from
God which humans waste
with conscious
indifference.

∞∞∞∞

The colors of nature reflect
in our soul and become the
prized perception of an
awakened mind. If we look
into reality with eyes open,
then beauty of the world is
all that we will find. The
wisdom in existence is
to free our spirit and live
life in truthful ways. Life
holds us in our true form,
spend time wisely with
every passing day.

Let There Be Wisdom in Truth

∞∞∞∞∞

The want of passion wills
our desires and transforms
us into the mold of existence.
The spirit bathes in the warmth
of nature's beauty and rinses
away from the dust of our
worldly substance. The blood
of humanity flows deep in
our veins and washes away
the stains of our conscious
mind. Pleasures of
life will burn the soul
and the wind will fan the
flames until nothing
is left behind.

∞∞∞∞∞

In our meditative state, we find
sanctuary in the deep reflective cave
of our eyes. We are created in our
dreams and write prose in
our blood, poetic beauty
eternalized. A flood of emotions
moves the pen to write verses
which the feeble heart can no
longer recognize. The wounds
of love cut deep into our longing,
where the pangs of love
never dies.

∞∞∞∞∞

Listen to the silent heartbeats as we
wait for the wind to bring her
fragrance to our door. Dear love, the
calm waves of emotions come into
the heart of love which we come to

adore. Why does the ocean
rush to the shore? The
will to love is the will of my
soul: her name is upon
my lips forevermore.

∞∞∞∞

Our eyes sleep into the night and
awaken in dreams which are
forevermore. Dawn's light comes
through our window and finds
us sleeping on the floor.
Consciousness rubs in our
eyes, as dreams escape
through the door.
Is it reality in dreams
or dreams in reality
which the mind
adores?

∞∞∞∞

Life journeys through unbroken time
when our footsteps become firm on
the ground in reality. Will we realize
in moments of reflection the vastness
of infinity? Filled with love of
wisdom, the spirit whispers to the
soul to surrender fully to the
beauty of nature. Will we bathe
in the river and immerse
in purity of water to
become the body
of creation?

∞∞∞∞

A heart was stolen by the spirit
of love and the only thing left in life
was pain in deep sorrow of

existence. Will we endure the storms of our emotions which are brewing in the body of our substance? True love is the path of life and becomes the luminous light which glows in our heart. Dear love, will you walk into our soul and become our beginning and end from the start?

∞∞∞∞

The simple truth of reality reflects in the mirror of consciousness, just open your eyes and see. Why do we fear the person we have become; the needs of the world will never set us free. Caught by the lure of power, humanity keeps following the same path to self-destruction. Wealth, greed, and vanity will hasten our end when we become blinded to our moral reflection.

∞∞∞∞

Hidden beauty is mystical and becomes a poetic vision to humanity with the passage of time. How far will we journey to find love and how high will we climb? Once the beauty of love is revealed, it is no longer beautiful to the heart. Love which lives in sensuous dreams holds us together to never break us apart.

Let There Be Wisdom in Truth

∞∞∞∞

The certainty of life is found in man's face when he is immersed in the truth of what he says. How humble is our will which seeks to move us toward our righteous ways? Consciousness holds our minds in a bowl of empty existence. True knowledge is to know the truth in wisdom which will become the roots of human intelligence.

∞∞∞∞

The ever-moving wind voices the mystical mood of the night. The eyes of the world drift into dreams, as consciousness looms in shades of light. Time moves like a river when we walk silently into the void of nonexistence. Will we ever see into our spirit the vision of reality which holds no substance?

∞∞∞∞

Oh quiet river, what makes you move so silently through the lush landscape of our watchful eyes? The body of your spirit reflects in our soul, and the purity of your reflection humbles the sky. Oh river, you bring life to all and quench the thirst of nature's

Let There Be Wisdom in Truth

existence. Your love for the
ocean is deep and strong
as you spread through the
heart of mighty earth
with graceful
persistence.

∞∞∞∞∞

Nature offers the heart of beauty and
a mystic poet takes it into her soul
with ecstasy. The oneness
of love is in the one we love which
becomes one with our destiny.
The unity of life is our breath of
existence which heaves with restless
emotions. The verses in poetic
moments are written
on scattered leaves held
to the wind by hands
of devotion.

∞∞∞∞∞

I have befriended my enemies;
they are now my most worthy of
friends. I have not forsaken my trust,
and they will honor me to my very
end. Forgiveness is one with
Christian virtue; to forgive is to
become human. Sacred wisdom is
the unconditional love that binds
man to woman. Call me what you
may but in God's morality, I will
not be betrayed. The human soul
lives and dies in the valor
of faith as into the hands
of danger I
have strayed.

∞∞∞∞∞

Imprisoned in the flesh of desires is the soul of our spiritual form. The web of existence is the iron will of reality which traps the mind in every norm. The purity of our spirit is stained by worldly greed. How deep we struggle to overcome our selfish nature and how shallow we become within our every need.

∞∞∞∞

The wings of freedom rise above the wind and take to the sky. The truth of existence is no heavy burden when the light of wisdom reflects in our eyes. A mind moves through time and soars in the deep vastness of consciousness. Will we ever awaken from dreams that hold no reality or ever touched by the spirit of righteousness?

∞∞∞∞

Let There Be Wisdom in Truth

∞∞∞∞∞

A mind becomes conscious when it
opens its doors to the light of true
perception. Does what we see truly
exists, is humanity riddled with
deception? The truth of self-
awareness is the mirror which
reflects the divine. A tender
spirit in love with nature
is most beautiful,
pure, and
sublime.

∞∞∞∞∞

The sands of time fall through
the hourglass as life takes its first
step to complete its thousand-mile
journey. Pressed in every grain are
the moments of existence endowed
to thee. The ground beneath our feet
is the story of life and the mind
writes what the mind wills to see.
Come home, oh bewildered soul,
you have walked too far into
the world; time makes
its final plea.

∞∞∞∞∞

What will we know when faced with
the truth of our mortality? True
wisdom is to make peace with
oneself and accept our fate in reality.
Time is infinite and moves toward
no end; the birth of life is its own
fatality. The beginning and end are
the walks of life, chasing the world
in vain banality. What will be gained
when we go against the will

of humanity? Human virtue
can no longer find a
home and wanders
in its world of
insanity.

∞∞∞∞

Dreams move deep into our
conscious soul and cleanse
the self from everyday existence.
The vision of reality fades with time
and loses the beauty of its essence.
Sleep is our moment of escape, as
the mind drifts in thoughts and
forgets all reason. The night
is most mystical, and
the world is all
freedom.

∞∞∞∞

The eternal truth is no theory
and will never test well. Does
it fail the empirical examination of
our free will? Only time will tell. The
wisdom of self-reflection
holds truth in faith and removes
the mask of deception from
the human race. The wheels
of life have many spokes,
but it's the axis of
truth which moves
us with grace.

∞∞∞∞

A fire which touches the soul
burns not. A heart which fans
the flames in ashes is caught.
Embers which glow with passion
rise in smoke and rub in a

Let There Be Wisdom in Truth

lover's eyes. The flames
of emotions remain
glowing long after
the fire dies.

∞∞∞∞

Oh Proud Age, we grow old too
quickly, but the spirit of youth still
clings to our soul, ageless and
timeless. The child within man
voices in our ears that life and death
are like rivers far-reaching and
endless. Time is written on withered
leaves and grows above the surface
of reality, only to fall back
to its roots of beginning.
Life moves in a circle of
time; every step is our
beginning and ends in
a world which will
keep spinning.

∞∞∞∞

True wisdom in happiness
is to let go the failures of
our shortcomings. The
pleasures of the world are
the web we weave, the soul
caught in its trapping. We
breathe in the air of the
world and chase dreams
scattered by the wind
far and wide. The
journey through life
is to walk back our
steps and leave
behind what
is outside.

∞∞∞∞

Mystical Fragrance

The morning light welcomes the mysteries of nature's radiance. Overwhelmed with love of sentiments, the flowers shed nature's calming mystical fragrance. Clouds in their dark gray mood drift over the forest and walk under the mountain peaks. The morning mist surrenders to the rising sun and sprinkles dust of dew on budding flowers' red rosy cheeks. Will we open our eyes to the wonders of this world and make our existence whole? The trees will hold their burden in stillness and nature will give us back our soul.

Birth of Spring

Spring sows the seeds of our existence and nature is most poetic and mystical in its graceful pose. Raindrops wash the world with great love and awaken the beauty of a slumbering rose. The hands of time embrace our dreams and pull us back into our core. Will we ever surrender our senses to the world and journey deeper into ourselves forevermore? The birth of spring grows in the light and colors of the world become

the soul of creation. Nature's eyes
have unveiled the hidden
beauty of love as our
hearts fills
with elation.

Soul of Humanity

Only through honest deeds
can truth obtain its moral virtue.
Our true nature is always kind,
generous, and will never hurt
you. Will we give to others what
we hold dear and precious in
our hearts? Humility is the
key to moral existence which
touches the soul of humanity
to make us human from the start.
It is only through compassion
that we can break through our
earthly form. Empathy binds
us to humanity and keeps
us calm in our
conscious storm.

Take Away

Take away hope from the world and it will grow dim in the light of darkness. Take away compassion from love and the world will grow heartless. Take away the spirit from our soul and the body will die without living. Take away the sweetness from our thirst and water will no longer be life-giving. Take away wisdom from man and he will grow old in youth. Take away hope from humanity and we will never strive in collective unity for the greater truth.

Crying Laughter

A life which is lived in dreams of imagination awakens the mind to a world of infinite possibilities. Will we breathe in our momentary existence and open our senses before the world passes us by? The music of life echoes in the heart of our soul as laughter makes us cry. Will we march into the heaviness of life and push against the burden of time?

A passing light is the ghost
of our laughter and the
tears of joy will
keep youth
sublime.

Guest for Life

A guest who comes into our
home is our guest for a day;
hospitality is a losing virtue
for the one who overstays.
Will we ever find a friend
who will become our guest
for life? The bond of
friendship can never be
broken even if we try
to cut it with a knife.
Who is it which keeps
knocking at our door?
He is a guest from God
who is most welcomed
whether rich or poor.

Moral Victory

A civilization which moves the
masses to act will overcome the
stagnation of history. A collective
vision of justice and truth will
overcome evil and lead humanity to
great moral victory. A conscious

soul mourns the body's blind will to
keep taking the poison of hate.
Will we ever listen to the voice of
reason and stop moving toward the
edge of our destructive fate? Is there
any good which comes of war but to
bring to surface the savagery of
human nature? Why do we keep
repeating the errors of history and
forget the moral wisdom
of our enlightened
teachers?

Wealth of Wisdom

The human spirit will not surrender
its love of freedom any more than
man's love for wealth. Human greed
will walk us toward every end until
we starve the life out of our health.
Deep are the pockets of our needs
which hold us heavy in our wisdom.
The true face of humanity no longer
mirrors God's true vision. The
treasures of the world
are earthly and corrosive to
our spirit. Those who hoard
will quicken their fall into
death: there is nothing
to gain in wealth
we inherit.

Nectar of Life

The vision of naked reality veils the conscious soul of man. What holds beauty in our eyes is the burning flames which beauty fans. Those who lust for love will burn in the flesh of their needs. True love is the sweet nectar of life upon which the spirit concedes. In the need to love, we become deeply faithful to the great joy of living. Compassion will become the heart of man only when the soul is all-giving.

Silent Words

Silent words which have not yet been spoken carry the greatest weight. The sweet pleasures of life become bitter when humanity loses its moral taste. True wisdom reflects our laughter to the world in reflecting ways. To seek life in our moments of passion is the journey the soul will come to praise. Meaningful existence will take us deep into life and give us all our earthly pleasures. What is happiness to the spirit, but a sense of contentment which we can't measure?

Water of Life

Knowledge walks into the door
of reason asking for the key to
wisdom in human existence.
In the deep abyss of time, the dust of
consciousness will settle in the
beauty of mind's essence. Are we
not but a drop in the deepest
of oceans and yet remain vain
still? How much water can
we hold in our hands which
gives life its fill? It is pure
silence which echoes Nature's
call to the wind. Will we see
the flowers of creation and
smell the fragrance of
spring which the
senses have
left behind?

Mirror of Truth

Naked reality will find the
one who hides in their clothes.
The face of pride looks at
the mask of deception with
a straight nose. Morality
will hold the mirror
which will reflect our only
truth to the world. The glass
reality will be shattered
into pieces with hate which
humanity hurls. Evil is
the soul of darkness which

light will never touch. A
mirror often reflects our
inner truth, but our
eyes will never see
it as such.

Let There Be Wisdom in Truth

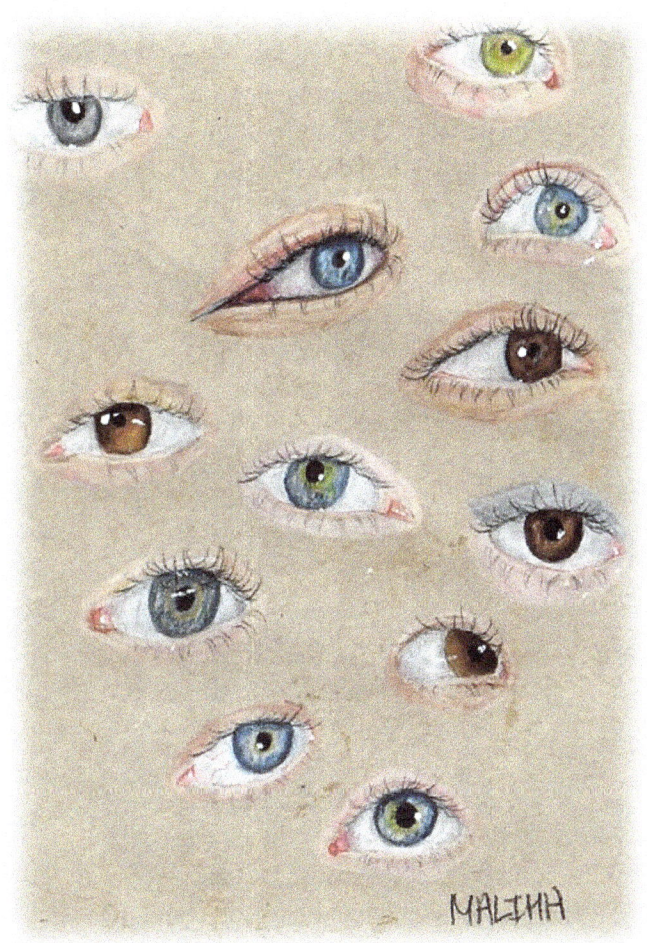

Searching Eyes

Born in the warmth of human comfort, we hope to break away and walk out into the world to play. A thousand-mile journey our lives will take, only to come back home to rest one day. Can we smell the splendor of nature's sensuous fragrance? Oh feeble heart, the journey through life is long, but aged wisdom will give its reverence. Will we remember our past as we walk into tomorrow with searching eyes? Human existence is but a lingering moment in time, eternity that never dies.

Heart of Giving

Fear not! Life will bring us into ourselves and will free us from the world of living. The wealth of the soul is the wisdom of love and the spirit is most enriched in the heart of giving. True happiness only comes to those who live with humble grace. A mirror will not reflect beauty when vanity is all that we see in our faces. The luxury of life is made empty when we amass wealth, only to impoverish our soul. We hoard our wealth,

only to dig our grave
to bury ourselves
whole.

Human Arrogance

The root of wisdom never grows
out from seeds of ignorance.
The purity of a child diminishes with
time and dies with arrogance. We
will grow old fast with time
if we only live for the outer world in
total blindness. A mind which
is full of pride becomes empty of
consciousness. Will we ever see
the reflection of light which
opens the world to our inner
truth? Human arrogance
does not age with wisdom
but remains bare in
our raw youth.

Endless Searching

Curiosity opens the imagination and
slips into our universe of ceaseless
searching. The human mind gets
tangled in its web of thought and
sets the trap in its reasoning. The
purpose of our existence and being
human is our intellectual reckoning.
A life without wisdom is like a

hopeless soul lost and wandering.
Will we let go of knowledge which
holds no purpose or meaning?
The mind will open our
eyes, but remains
lost in endless
searching.

Life's Circle

Memories age with time and
move us farther and farther away
from our childhood. Youth ripens
with wisdom when the child grows
into manhood. The circle of
life will bring us back to our
childish beginning. Like
a river which moves into
the ocean, we grow
old with time by
moving around
the wholeness
of living.

Wisdom of Insight

If humanity has done no wrong
to the righteousness of existence,
then it must be our consciousness
which has done us wrong. The
human spirit is the moral fiber
of our being; even when pulled

by the strong, will it remain strong? Human virtue is the blood of our soul which gets spilled when we bleed our hearts with hate. Why do we burn the spirit with fiery emotions and simmer in the embers of our fate? The face of anguish can no longer hide our form when the light shines on it bright. Why live with ignorance when faith has given us the wisdom of insight?

Good of Humanity

It is only through the eyes of wisdom that we can wash away our darkness. It is only through ever empowering of love that we can bring compassion into the heartless. Will humans ever sacrifice their souls for the greater good of humanity? It is our pride that will not free us from the shackles of our vanity. Let the blood flow into our veins and move us closer to the conscious spirit of living. Those who are truly wise hold no hate, no anger; they are compassionate and all-forgiving.

Will to Power

Power wills truth to conform to its will to power and holds captive the human race. We have no love in our hearts and the rhythm of life has lost its pace. We walk endlessly searching for happiness here, there, and every place. Why do we run in circles chasing the wind trying to hold it in empty space? Humanity becomes oppressed by evil only when power oppresses human grace. The eyes of wisdom hold no sight when power puts a veil over our face.

Will to Conform

The spirit of self-realization cuts into the web of reality and escapes with conscious awareness. Breathe in our moments of freedom until the wisdom of existence holds us breathless. The vastness of human virtue is no bigger than the human heart. Moral courage is a cowardly act if we remain quiet and don't take part. It is the spirit

which liberates the soul
from the surface of our
worldly form. The cloth
which covers our naked
truth no longer
hides our will
to conform.

Love Within

The deep thirst for living
cannot fulfill our shallow
desires which remain infinite.
What is the purpose of life
which comes into being and
becomes love's most intimate?
Blindly we search for the
one we love but never
realize she hides behind
our bewildering eyes. True love
will make you feel mystical;
if you come too close, charm will
die. We journey through time
in search of beauty to find
the love we fashion. We walk
in steps of heavy emotions,
holding the burden
in our over-bearing
passion.

Life's Center

The great steps in time move
the center of life's existence and
bend the will of humanity to be
fully realized. The voice of wisdom
calls the spirit to look straight into
the world to see the self which is no
longer recognized. Nature will hold
our face to reality, deep in thought
of mystical wonder. The colors
of the world are imbued in
poetic dreams and give life
their glowing splendor. How
quickly time runs from our
youth and how quickly we
weather through the ages.
A journey through life
is the flickering
moments in time which
we sift through like
slow-turning
pages.

Whirling Dance

Why wander in all directions
when we all will come to one road of
understanding? Pressed under the
sound of our voice, words move the
spirit and the melody of emotions
breathes in our soulful chanting. The
rhythm of nature moves us to dance
and lifts our hands upward into the
sky. The whirling dance is our

circle of life which moves us
deeper into the conscious
eye. Time escapes through
our hands as we run too
fast in life. We are cut
into fragmented moments
by the edge of reality,
sharper than
any knife.

Shallow Soul

Delusions of the world have
been revealed and live in the
the perception of our illusions.
A mind in a haze of confusion
can hold no truth and can
reach no conclusions.
Stagnation moves us not,
but move we must to
overcome our stagnation.
Creation improves us not, but to
improve we must overcome
our creation. It is the conscious
will which drowns the soul in
shallow rivers, shallow
streams. Is the reality
of existing real to the eye
which lives under
the semblance
of dreams?

Let There Be Wisdom in Truth

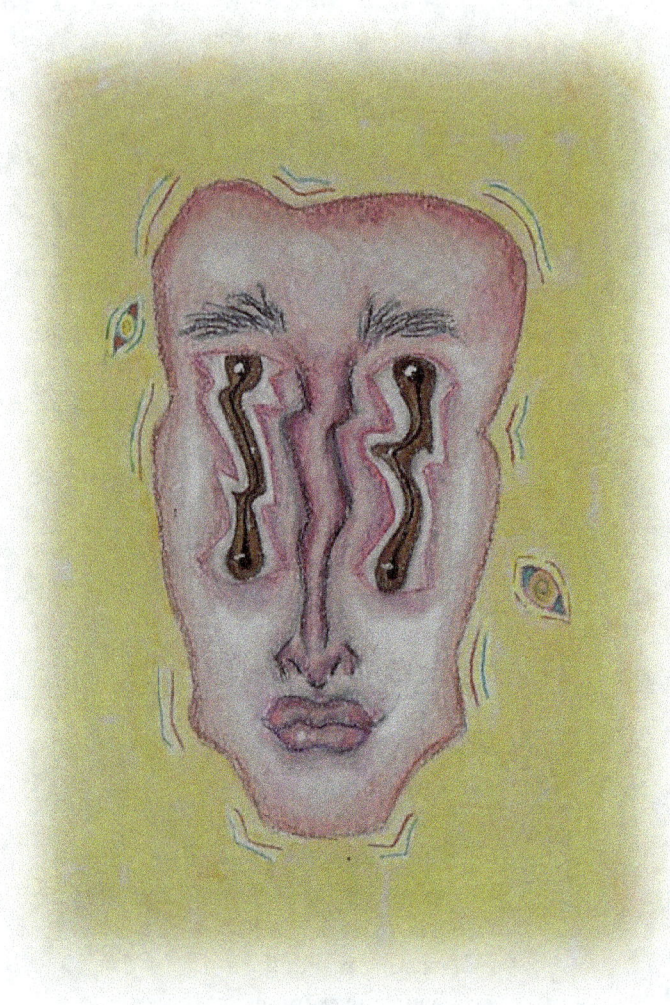

Walls of Time

Savagery is the evolutionary character of humanity which keeps pulling us back to our primitive past. Civility is the heart of a nation when morality comes into consciousness fast. The walls of time stand strong only to crumble under the weight of our stubborn will. Empires rise and fall for human glory to build, destroy with war and skill. Good can only overcome evil when we hold the courage to face our darkness. Truth is the character of our civilization which enlightens the spirit with radiance and brightness.

Blind Faith

The great loss of mortal Man is not to ask for God's forgiveness and grace. The guilt of being human has made us guilty in a faith which reflects our blind face. Why do we keep washing our sins in holy water which is no longer holy? The soul mourns the death of morality and sheds bloody tears in melancholy. Will we overcome the rituals in blind faith and open our eyes to the light of God? We take

pride in our perfection,
but in God's infinite
purity man is
stained and
flawed.

Human Pride

The will of human imagination gave
birth to our beginning and bears
witness to man's glory. It is the
illusion of human immortality which
is the arrogance of our never-
ending story. The path of humanity
has spanned the Earth and is etched
in every corner of time. We hold the
world in our hands, but it is the pride
of being human which hinders
our upward climb. The soul
of humanity was born in its
spiritual form by nature's
loving hands. Human
wisdom has freed our
spirit and the power of
our mind dominates
the sky, the ocean,
and all virgin
lands.

Sacred Gift

God created man to live through man: the end of man is the end of God. The fate of humanity will take us to the end of time, but we must first bow to infinity with a humble nod. The will to conquer Nature has taken humanity over vast trails to walk under peaked mountains. Why pursue immortality and consume our lives seeking life's magic fountain? We build to destroy and destroy to build the vision of our destructive ways. Life is a sacred gift from God: we can have it for a moment, but can quickly be swept away.

Human Banality

It is the fault of the conscious mind which convinces humanity of their sacred fate in reality. Man's ego is the stench of civilization and smells too much of human banality. The savage nature of power has taken humanity through the darkest times in history. The blood of consciousness spills, and morality mourns its death in pain and misery. The voice of reason has awakened our

mind and gives humanity
the vision to go beyond
the senses. Will we open
our heart to the world
and let go of all our
defenses? Knowledge
of nature has liberated
our spirit, but knowing
too much is our trap
with dangerous
consequences.

Blind Greed

The epic of human history has
been written with the blood
of a poor man's soul. Power holds
the might of Man as he hoards
treasures which can't fill his bowl.
The well of pleasure is too deep;
there is no bottom, no surface to
our needs. We are consumed by
our existence chasing empty
dreams which hasten our end
with speed. The opulence of
the world will make us blind
and measly in our living.
The rich will hide their
wealth, but it is the
poor man's heart
which is made
rich by giving.

Wish to See

It is the eyes of the world that unveil the truth which humans no longer wish to see. The night's darkness spreads into the conscious soul and the spirit wanders on its endless sea. How beautiful is life's wisdom which helps us see our foolish ways? How will we walk through darkness when our vision has gone astray?

Water in Bowl

The blind will open their eyes, but cannot see beyond their blindness. Truth will hold our light and wash away our darkness. A mind opens its conscious eye to look deep into its soul. We come to fill our thirst by holding our water in our bowl. If we look at the world with open eyes, then we will see our true reflection. The mirrors of reality are surface deep, but hold us in our true perception.

Eyes Closed

The rule of law is to uphold peace and justice. It is the powerful which writes the words of its substance. Humanity can't find purpose in existence when they walk the world with their eyes closed. The road is long, and our journey is limited by what time has imposed. The poor will bear the hardships of life with their quiet humble stare. If we hold our moral virtue, then truth will find us everywhere.

Time Lost

Beauty lost in washed away time looks on passing moments with glassy eyes. The vigor of youth once ran in our blood but is now a flickering light which fades and dies. The sparks of time have turned to ashes and silent emotions are left in flames. Oh, ever-moving time, we beg of you to give us more and, even near death, we keep calling for your name. There are moments when life dims our eyes so we can hide our sullen faces from our moral state. We have become string-puppets in the drama of life and play the role in the hand of fate.

Bridge to Reality

A bridge is half-finished, and
the mind half-fulfilled in the journey
towards a full sense of its wholeness
in creation. Humanity will look
beyond time and wander in
search of self-realization. The world
has gone blind; there is too much
glare in our eyes to see our noble
face. The bridge to reality will
crumble with time and our
footsteps will move far into
life with wisdom
and grace.

Run Free

The heaviness of life is made light
by the wings of freedom. Take
flight, oh feeble heart, we have
broken the walls of our human
kingdom. A spirit runs free
under the landscape of the
open sky. Will humans ever
touch the fire which burns
in their inner eye? Our
soul has forgotten the words
of wisdom which fall deep
into the abyss of silence.
In our consciousness, human
morality runs free and in
the spirit of our freedom
there is no injustice,
tyranny, or
violence.

Golden Rule

Seek justice, not the jewel;
be just in action and follow
the golden rule. The treasures
we seek can only be found within.
Will humanity ever find pleasure in
wealth which is built on mortal
sin? If we live in our moral
way, then we will find
the truth in the
light of day.

Selfish Genes

The laws for the rich are a
poor man's fool. True justice
will reign over the powerful
who rule. Caught in the
web of our existence, we
become trapped in deep-
rooted dreams. It is our
fierce nature which cloaks
us in our selfish genes.
Blind in power, we oppress
our soul with endless
greed. Humanity holds
no power, but makes us
powerful when we
are selfless
in our deeds.

Hour to Toil

A body lays on the surface of reality
and the soul is the essence of our
human form. Desires rich in
sentiments will run through the heart
to calm our inner emotional storm.
How can we find peace in a world
which is full of disarray and turmoil?
We run to our center and the
pendulum of reality will move
back and forth in our hour of toil.
It is the love of truth which makes
us whole. The reflection of our
beauty has become the
vision of our soul.

Firm Ground

Life is born into the moment
and grows into the world like
an aged tree consciously rooted
in time. Youthful steps run
far into the open fields, but
in old age, hard is the climb.
How far and deep will we look
into life and come to realize
that there is so much we can't
see? Close your eyes to look inside
your soul and there all shall be.
We journey toward the truth in
search of wisdom and walk
firm on the ground under our
steps. Memories wander
into our mind as our eyes
trace back lost time
in fading footsteps.

Humble Submission

Man's sober reality is pride in his intellectual craving for the light of recognition. The will of the mind is set free to pursue great love of ideas with full volition. The deeper we go into knowledge, the less wisdom will come to fruition. How much purpose can a man gain when life's goal is self-ambition? Why perplex the mind with complexity when the nature of reality is beyond human cognition? We hold the spirit under the tyranny of inquisition when humanity cannot bow in humble submission?

Truthful ways

Human consciousness strives for greatness, but gets caught in their trap of contradiction. The temptation of fame imprisons the mind under the will of heart's conviction. Destiny awaits, as the imprints of our footsteps trace the forgotten moments of our history. Were we not born to wonder and ponder on our existence, veiled in a cloud of human mystery? The secrets of humanity will never

be told in truthful ways.
Housed in walls of human
nature is our sheer vanity
which wisdom will
never praise.

Savage Nature

A soul of man's spirit lingers
in the firmness of his features.
The power of his mind conquered
the world, and yet he cannot shed
his savage nature. The wealth of the
world he will built with great pride.
Deeper and deeper he digs into his
greedy ways until the walls of time
close him from all sides. Humanity
has walked far into civilization but
still can't reach life's doorsteps. Man
will buffer the evils of passions
as wisdom tries to hold
firm his footsteps.

Conscious Perception

It is jealousy in our character
which makes us prisoner in our
existence. Envy of what can
and cannot be is an illusion of
perception which can't hold any
substance. Morality will never take
root unless the human spirit seeks

wisdom through justice. Moral goodness is lost to the world, we believe; the universal truth is just us. The purpose of living is wasted with time when we hide behind the veil of deception. How can we see the world with eyes which have not looked into conscious perception?

Spiritual Journey

Courage will hold us in doubt if we run away from the hardships of life. The easy road is straight and wide, but filled with endless strife. Curiosity is our deep wonder into life which binds us to the mind's creative will. How tragic is our love for humanity when it is the heart of our lover which we kill. Our steps become heavy, when heavy doubts ramble in our restless mind. A spiritual journey through life holds no meaning if the road to self-realization we no longer can find.

Walls of Silence

A quiet home warms the human spirit and is a comfort to our eyes. A candle's eye blankets us from the world of darkness where the heart's light never dies. The walls of silence stand still with time as we reflect in the consciousness of our existence. How long will we hide behind the truth of living and destroy our moral essence? A stranger comes knocking at our door and we will listen and wonder. Our home stands motionless on the roof over our existence to hide us under.

Conscious River

The still water of our dream world reality is the deep well of our soul. A thirst for existence lies in a hand full of water which makes the spirit whole. Water will reflect the face of humanity in the purity of our emotions. Will we walk toward our conscious river which moves under our feet silently in slow motion? Can we hold our vision deep into our awareness and let our life flow like an ever-moving river?

We are but a drop in
the ocean flowing
into the heart of
one who is
our Giver.

Oh, Solitude

Oh solitude, you have not yet found me at home. Written words will not come to the surface with these unspoken poems. The beauty of life's wisdom wanders in the mind's eye, like a mystic poet walking into her soul. She carries the love for God deep in her spirit, begging for salvation in her empty bowl. Will she voice in our ears the spirit of nature's laughter? Washed in colors and hue of emotions, the verses of poetry will search for her heart forever-after.

Deep Rooted

Nature shall deceive us not in simple joys which Nature brings. Life is but a moment of passing; time is rooted in all things. The seeds of reality have been sown in our soul and we will

take them back into our
grave. Were we not molded
into clay by the spiritual
water that we crave? The
sediments of reality settle
in our dreams and form
life's silver pearl. We are
born deep-rooted
to life and to live as
guests of
this world.

Stillness of Life

We can fight against our
will, but it is our nature that
goes against the ways of our
spirit. Born human, we walk
into the world with moral eyes that
we inherit. Wisdom will keep us
humble and mindful of our fragile
existence. The farther we walk away
from ourselves, the more time we
need to cover the distance. In the
stillness of life, we move through
time on so many roads, so many
ways. Our journey is etched in
our footsteps: life walks with
time, the joy of living
houses our nights
and days.

The Spirit Escapes

The birth of human emotions
grows with our moments of
existence in myriad ways. Divine
light casts no shadow, but gives us
our role in worldly plays. The
vastness of infinity is beyond timely
existence. How long will time travel
into eternity to realize its conscious
essence? A child's wisdom will only
show when a man grows into
the child. The human
spirit has escaped into the
world and walks
free and wild.

Mocking Laughter

The voice of mocking laughter
fans the flames of human folly.
Listen not to your heart's emotions,
but reason's true calling. Great is
wisdom which gives meaning to
words less spoken. The wind walks
empty-handed but leaves human
arrogance unbroken. Truth is
revealed to those who give their
mind to the world of mystery.
Will we ever overcome
the dangers of pride,
the fateful story of
human history?

Toward Salvation

Oh, voice of morality, you have
awakened the truth of our existence.
Will you sever us from our carnal
emotions and break the
iron will of indifference? Oh,
humanity, were you not born
by the love of God's grace,
only to fall from a great height
of arrogance? How shallow we live
on the surface of time, only the truth
in wisdom can reveal the depth of
our ignorance. Will we
walk the hard road toward
salvation which we can shorten
the great distance? Human
dignity is in the eyes of
humanity and reflects
the beauty of
God's essence.

Withered Leaves

The circle of life bends with
time and takes us back to
our beginning. Oh, humanity,
darkness has fallen upon
our eyes; are we conscious or
still dreaming? Awake, oh
spirit awake and listen to
the sound of nature's calling.
Withered leaves cling
helplessly to their existence
in time, humanity clings to

their grace which keeps
falling. Truth will reflect
in the darkness of our eyes
and glow in the light of our
conscious mind. The
journey through life
begins with time; like
guests, we come
and go from this
world to leave
everything
behind.

One Moment

There is one moment, and no
other moments, to bring our
lives back into the moment.
We have walked forward, and
then backward, giving our
spirit no room for movement.
Our minds will take us deep into
thought to seek and search for our
creative will. The beauty of the
world is divine love infused with
colors which poetry distills. Why do
we burden life with things which
hold too much weight, if lifting
the spirit is what we
prefer? If we run blind,
then life will move too
fast with time
and become
a continuous
blur.

Broken Seam

The day has awakened, but we are
still asleep in our dreams. Are we
but a dream in reality, a broken
stitch of perception torn at the seams?
The soul moves into the world
looking for meaning in the wisdom
of true living. Thirst for pleasures
will drown the spirit and leads
to great sorrow, woeful and
unforgiving. Our conscious
eyes awaken and the body
walks into our spirit reborn.
The veil of humanity holds
us blind until the mask
of reality is torn.

Circle of Existence

The circle of existence takes us
from our beginning toward our
end, and then brings us back
to our beginning. Those who strive
for fame, wealth, and power run
around in circles hoping to stop time
from spinning. Let it go, the feeble
heart keeps telling, but we become
tangled in our never-ending greed. Will
we ever go beyond ourselves and
find the courage to act in our moral
deeds? Why waste the whole of
existence searching for treasures
which we can never find?
The grains of time keep

falling into our hands
holding onto
them blind.

Veil of Life

Will we breathe in the joy of life
to let go of our world of being?
We search for the truth but
what we find is the veil of
deception in our living. Look
into the mirrors of our eyes
and we will only see the lines
of our face. Does humanity
have the courage to speak
against the banality of our
race? Such is the way
of life as we wander blindly
on the surface of reality.
Will we shine light
on darkness of
which we
can't see?

Let There Be Wisdom in Truth

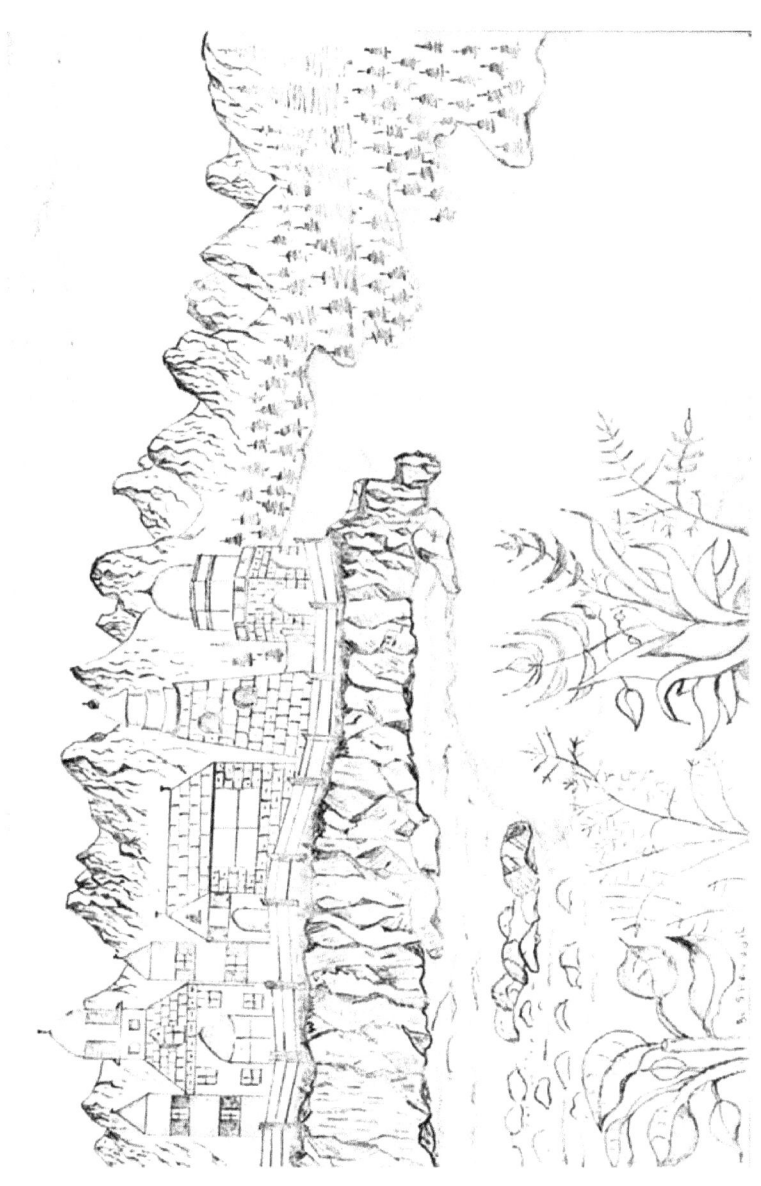

Wisdom in Truth

The eyes of humanity have no
face and see no light in virtue
to overcome evil. The corrupt
nature of man is the power
which leads to destruction
and upheaval. To conquer
and to be conquered is the
lunacy of war most medieval.
The evolution of human
history is intellectually
primordial and
primeval.

∞∞∞∞∞

The spirit is a gift to the soul
and the body is a well to worldly
pleasures. How vast is our reach
and how infinite our dreams,
when even time can't measure? All
will come, and all will go; the
universe is beyond grasp.
Why run to and from
chasing the wind, in
breathless gasp?

∞∞∞∞∞

The divine nature of beauty is
simple, but no longer reflects the
vision of human grace. The light has
washed away man's subtle form and
the words of true wisdom have been
erased. What does heaven hold for
us when we are mere mortals
trapped in our mortality? The
secrets of living are the miracle
of existence, filled with

distilling emotions in
our spirituality.

∞∞∞∞

The truth of words is powerful, only
to the ears which are willing to hear.
Words which escape in heat of
emotions can erase good deeds of
many years. Think before you speak
and be thoughtful in your wisdom
before you voice your words to
the wind. Compassion gives
solace to words and
brings humility into
a cultivated
mind.

∞∞∞∞

Silent undertones are music to the
soul; to hear it we must listen to it
with stillness in our heart. Oh
silence, what is it that you speak of
which holds our spirit apart? It is
moments of realization to which
our mind listens to, as wisdom
in our thoughts is what we
impart. Will we hear the
beauty of our words
which uplift the soul
from the start?

∞∞∞∞

The misfortunes of life bring
strength to our soul and become the
wisdom to overcome our weakness.
We house treasures of the world
which make us rich but bring the
soul nothing but emptiness. The

Let There Be Wisdom in Truth

hardship of life moves the spirit to
grow and live. True happiness
comes to those who take
nothing but in spirit
always give.

∞∞∞∞

A light which glows in our spirit
becomes the vision of truth in our
eyes. What are the coverings of
conscious reality where only
wisdom lies? A river moves in the
heart of the world as a mirror
to the sky. Are we moving
toward our destiny, seeking
the purpose and meaning
of life before we die?

∞∞∞∞

We are touched by true love
which burns with emotions,
so sweet is the pain. True
love only comes once,
and then will never
come again. We are
in love, forever in love
when we surrender to
love's mystical charm.
To die for love is noble
and does the
spirit no harm.

∞∞∞∞

Listen! Do we hear the soft voice of
nature telling us to open the window
into our soul? What will it take to
feel the moment, and touch with our
lips nature's bowl? The melody

of sound holds the wind in
rapture, and the symphony
of music becomes the spirit
of nature. The echo of deep
mystery has awakened
the conscious mind
as the mystical
spirit becomes
our loving
teacher.

∞∞∞∞

The thirst for water reflects our face
of needs and holds us shallow on the
reflected surface. It is the eyes of
reality that open our vision to see the
wisdom of our humble grace. Once
thirst for life is fulfilled, then
drinking more water will drown us
in our drunken state. Arrogance is
the excess of human greed,
never enough, no matter
how big the plate.

∞∞∞∞

Let There Be Wisdom in Truth

∞∞∞∞

The glory of morning lifts the
veil from our conscious eyes
and warms the spirit in serenity of
light. The colors of the world cling
to the senses and nature's beauty is
mind's delight. Time holds
our emotions in the heart
of youth and the beauty of
the world is nature at play.
Oh life, you are a gift to
our existence and a
moment of rapture
in the light
of day.

∞∞∞∞

We hold hands to give each
other our sacred souls. The
spirit of love grows in our hearts
and the fragments of existence
become whole. The light from
our inner emotions washes
away darkness from our
eyes. In our embrace
is serenity of the world
where the spirit of
truth in eternity
never dies.

∞∞∞∞

If we follow our dreams into the
twilight of night, then time will hold
us in the stillness of light. Will
we ever awaken from our
dreams and live the life that
we have dreamed? Was it

a dream that we dreamed
or a dreamed reality
that it seemed?

∞∞∞∞

In deep searching thoughts burns the mind which seeks curiosity which escapes perception. Our eyes tell the story of truth in reality, but consciousness holds our body in deception. True knowledge sheds light into wisdom and moves us deeper into life's mystical ways. Time walks under our feet and the footsteps of our journey are molded by mud and clay.

∞∞∞∞

The power of will is what wills us to power against our will. The blood of humanity which we spill is the hands of power that we distill. The want of power is the pride of man which man guards with great skill. Lost in the world of vanity, power consumes the soul that it kills.

∞∞∞∞

Naked passion clothed in cravings becomes the mystical lure for the ravenous spirit. Caught in a web of life, the soul is trapped, but humanity chooses not to escape it. The soul will give no love when the heart is lost in the pleasures of the world. What holds our feet

Let There Be Wisdom in Truth

is the anguish of being
mortal which makes
our spirit whirl.

∞∞∞∞∞

We drift on the river of dreams,
caught in a storm of emotions. Why
wake up to the real world of
certainty which no longer gives love
to devotion? Lost in fast-paced
time, life is a vision in memory of
our reflection in slow motion.
How deep is the surface
of our dream, how
deep is the ocean?

∞∞∞∞∞

The night holds us in our
dreams as the world fall
quietly to sleep. The eyes of
reality watch over us and
time is a treasure for us to
keep. In the depth of our
existence, the mind reflects
on the coming of morning
light. Awakened by
sounds of distant birds
our consciousness slips
through the veil
of night.

∞∞∞∞∞

Let There Be Wisdom in Truth

∞∞∞∞∞

Thoughts come to mind, but the
moral voice holds them silent.
Words can have a bitter taste, harsh
aftertaste, and can become violent.
Will we hold them from coming into
our spirit which they want to overtake?
The light of wisdom will wash
away evil once our moral
consciousness
is awake.

∞∞∞∞∞

The human spirit traces its
vision into the past as his eyes
reflect on distant forgotten
dreams. Memories are imprints
of time, and eternity is but a
night it seems. How fast life
moves through time, like a
stream of glimmering light
bending and swerving in
bodily motion. Moments
are buried into our
existence, layered
in our eyes, the
memories of
etched emotions.

∞∞∞∞∞

How deep is true love which no
emotion can bring to the surface of
our heart? Can we ever look
into a poet's deep-felt eyes and
embrace her words before they part?
The colors of life are imbued in
nature's all-encompassing

grace. Will we walk into the
world with silent steps,
and slow down in our
worldly pace?

∞∞∞∞

The spirit is awakened by the
sound of the wind and becomes
the symphony of music for
the heart. Will we allow conscious
moments to take us into our joy of
being and bring color to our world
from the start? The simplicity
of nature's beauty touches
the soul with tranquility of
light. In purity of existence,
nature's beauty is pristine to
our uplifting pleasures
which soar to
great height.

∞∞∞∞

A winter storm is consumed by
the wind as snow falls like cotton,
glazing the world in white milky
frost. The virgin landscape is cold
and unforgiving in which the soul of
nature is lost. Trees bear their silent
frozen state and carry their heavy
burden with humbled
pride. The eyes of spring
have not yet awakened
and the bitterness of
winter's glory
embraces us
from all sides.

∞∞∞∞

Let There Be Wisdom in Truth

∞∞∞∞

The sun reflects its light upon the moon and the moon's mystical glow reflects upon the world. In the darkness of night, the two lovers move in their binding dance, one pulls, the other is hurled. Oh, stars of the night, your sparkling glory is everlasting, but it is your far-reaching mystery which sustains your existence. How great is the sun's golden light which touches the soul of nature from so far a distance?

∞∞∞∞

Love walks in quietly and marches with graceful rhythm into our hearts. Never-ending dreams linger in our emotions like drifting time which never pulls us apart. The purity of love reflects the beauty of life in eyes that live for their true meaning. We lose our existence in time the moment we drift further into our dreaming.

∞∞∞∞

Let There Be Wisdom in Truth

Will we nourish the soul with the sweet fruit of wisdom? Time will hold our mind, but it is the conscious perception which will give us our freedom. The colors of nature are infinite shades, filled with mystical beauty. The human form is our body of existence which houses the spirit of our being. Our conscious eye will unveil the mask from worldly reality. Will we ever look into the world, to know, and find our hidden morality?

I Am I

Fear me not, I am the hidden truth that lurks in the darkness of your soul. Look at me not in the mirror of conscious reflection, for I am the real face behind the mask of humanity. Hold me not as a slave of worldly needs, for I am the caged bird that sings your praise. Move me not against my will, for I am the hand that writes the words of your destiny. See me not, for I am the light that blinds the eyes which seek divine wisdom. I hold the power over good and evil. I fear no one, but the one who holds too much pride in their heart.

All truths are like rivers which flow through me. I am the deep well of human passion that keeps mankind thirsty. I am the mind of the universe and infinity is the simple act of my intellectual will. I am the sword which cuts through the flesh of life to reveal the wounds of human suffering. I am the hand which moves the wind far into the world. I am the blood of civilization which runs through the heart of human nature. I am the mother of all existence and all of existence exists through me. I am the shadow of human form and the light in the soul of darkness. I am happiness within sorrow and sorrow within happiness. I am the footsteps of humanity which walk through your door. I am

Let There Be Wisdom in Truth

the virtue in morality and morality is
the essence of my nature. I am the
spirit of spirituality and there
are no walls in my kingdom.
I am within and I am without.
I am nothing and I am
everything in your being.

I have no home, but I live in a
heart of love and compassion. I
am the fire which you can't touch,
but I will give you comfort and
warmth in your bitter cold world. I
am the bridge between heaven and
earth; I can walk you toward the
path of righteousness. I am
the spark in your dreams and
the splendor of morning light. I
am the soul which is eternal
like a mist of twilight
that glows in the
mystical night.

Let There Be Wisdom in Truth

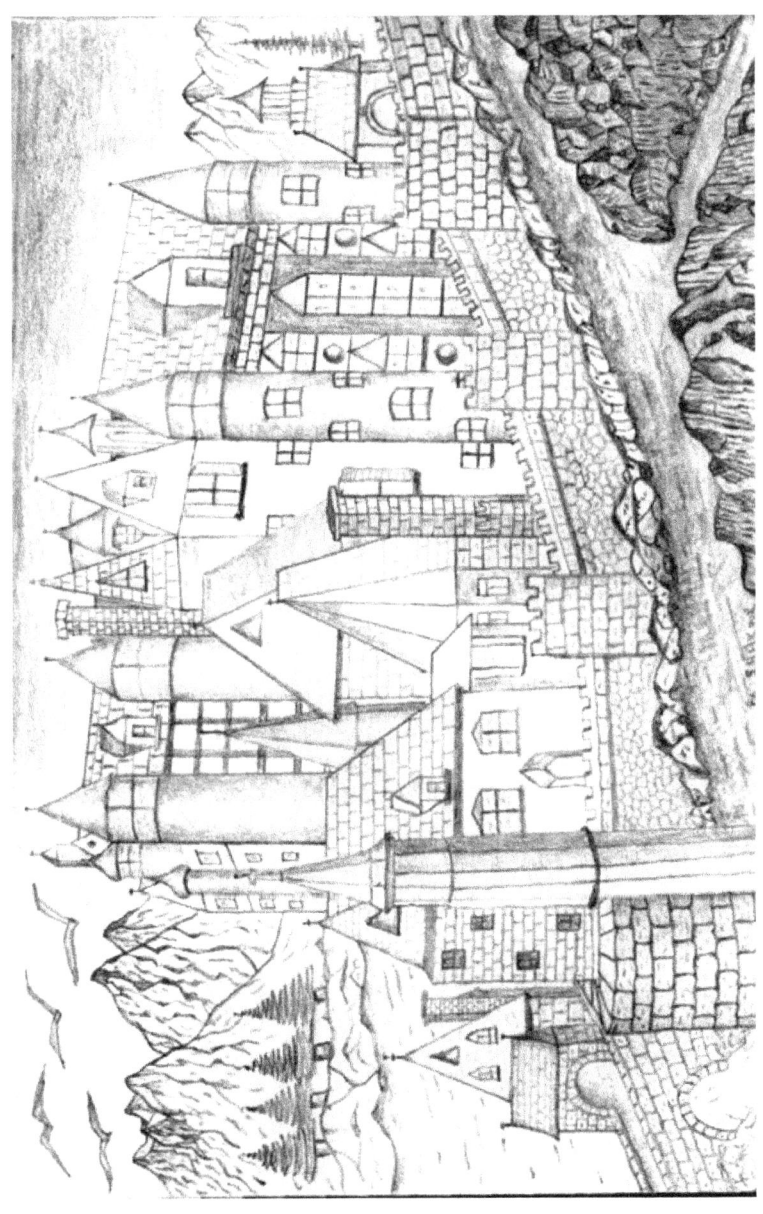

The Climb

The eyes of nature open into spring's sacred truth. We come into the first of time as we learn to grow in our tender youth. A mind only finds peace when it seeks salvation in a beggar's bowl. A world is full of colors which give solace to the conscious soul. The lifestory of humanity is written on pages of time. A journey through life is steep, but a strong will to move will ease the climb.

Wealth

If we share our wealth and give some to the poor then we become rich in spirit, need no walls, and need no doors. The humble soul holds no value for the wealth of this world. Lost in the pleasures of life, the heart is darkened when reason is hurled. Will we ever chase the wind, which is gentle and sweet? The richness of life is our simple journey which moves us under our feet.

Steps in Life

A path into time will take a thousand steps and will cross hundreds of roads. The burden of existence is heavy with needs, but our stubborn will carry the load. We are under the grace of our conscious existence. Time keeps us captive only when we give ourselves to blind ambivalence. The hand of God is gracious, visible to the one who seeks the wisdom to know. Come into me and unburden your burden with love I will sow.

Enter

The spirit of God is the candle's eye which glows into our heart. What are these embers of emotions which burn in life from the start? Let us breathe out our conscious moments and take in the wisdom of life with every breath. Life is a gift like no other; it is yours from beginning till death. If we live in our worldly storm, then there will be no calm in our spiritual center. Will we open our conscious soul and give wisdom a door to enter?

Soul of Spring

The wind moves softly in humble steps and whispers to the soul of Spring. Will you break open the boundaries of this world and let freedom fly under your wings? The face of reality has opened its eyes and seek the moral truth. The spirit is in love with nature's beauty and lives in the spirit of youth. Nature is the hope for humanity, and everything is but a broken dream. The coming of spring washes away the worldly dust and becomes a moving river in our conscious stream.

Final Word

We stir our imagination to give wings to love's eternal form. Can we break the will of enduring time and bring harmony into our searching eyes? Will we reflect our dreams on the surface of reality and bring them to consciousness in our truthful ways? The world will keep us in our moments of solace. We must remain virtuous in actions and move toward a life of simplicity. A burst of laughter echoes in our hearts and the spacious sound will awaken the sleeping soul. Tears of rapture reflected in our eyes to give us the courage to take in our sorrow.

The time we lose will never come back to us, but it will give us the wealth of wisdom we hope to gain. Days and nights will slip through our minds like the splendor of youth lost to the ages. Pressed in every grain of time are the footsteps of our journey, washed away by every drop of our existence. We have come to live in the shadow of our being and the light will become our body of comfort. The purity of the world holds our vision and the eyes of humanity long to take in the colors and beauty of nature. The voice of reason will awaken our spirit; the hands of time will give comfort to the desolate soul.

Let There Be Wisdom in Truth

How can we liberate ourselves without becoming worldly prisoners in our fleeting existence? Have we become the dust in reflected light wandering in the vastness of eternity? Will we take in the moment of awareness to let the sensuous breeze embrace our soul? Life's fragrance filters into our consciousness and dissolves our emotions in sacred water. The joy of our spirit opens to children at play. Can we ever become children once more to cleanse away the layers of our conscious world? Will we ever find ourselves in the flickering memories of withering time? How can we shed the sorrow of living when the heaviness of life seems so burdensome? Can we breathe in the breath of faith and breathe out the air of uncertainty? Freedom is our virtue of being happy and true happiness is the virtue of being free.

Let there be wisdom in truth. Let there be truth in wisdom. Let there be light in wisdom. Let there be wisdom in light. Let there be hope in humanity. Let there be humanity in virtue. Let there be joy in sorrow. Let there be great love for today to give it to the world tomorrow.

∞∞∞∞

Let There Be Wisdom in Truth

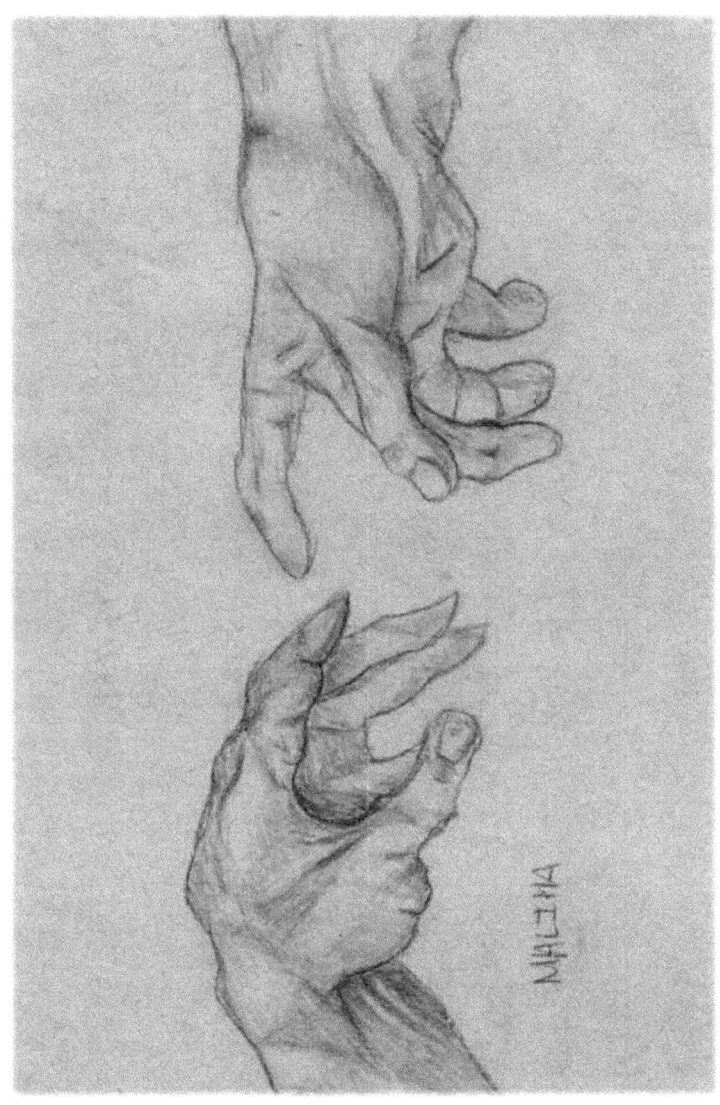

www.ingramcontent.com/pod-product-compliance
Lightning Source LLC
Chambersburg PA
CBHW070232230426
43664CB00014B/2274